Simply Amazing
Spiral Quilts

By RaNae Merrill

kp

CINCINNATI, OHIO

mycraftivity.com

CONNECT. CREATE. EXPLORE.

Other fine Krause Publications titles are available from your local bookstore, craft supply store, online retailer or visit our website at www.fwpublications.com.

12 11 10 09 08   5 4 3 2 1

Distributed in Canada by Fraser Direct
100 Armstrong Avenue
Georgetown, ON, Canada L7G 5S4
Tel: (905) 877-4411

Distributed in the U.K. and Europe by David & Charles
Brunel House, Newton Abbot, Devon, TQ12 4PU, England
Tel: (+44) 1626 323200, Fax: (+44) 1626 323319
E-mail: postmaster@davidandcharles.co.uk

Distributed in Australia by Capricorn Link
P.O. Box 704, S. Windsor NSW, 2756 Australia
Tel: (02) 4577-3555

Library of Congress Cataloging-in-Publication Data

Merrill, RaNae.
  Simply amazing spiral quilts / by RaNae Merrill. -- 1st ed.
    p. cm.
  Includes index.
  ISBN 978-0-89689-653-6 (pbk. : alk. paper)
  1. Patchwork--Patterns. 2. Quilting--Patterns. 3. Spirals in art. I.
Title.
  TT835.M4793 2008
  746.46'041—dc22
                          2008017314

Production edited by Amy Jeynes and Sarah Laichas
Designed by Amy F. Wilkin
Production coordinated by Matt Wagner

About the Author

RaNae Merrill found her calling as a quilter after previous careers as a professional pianist, a photographer and a travel writer. These days she satisfies her wanderlust by traveling to quilt shows and guilds as a teacher and lecturer. She has designed fabrics for Blank Quilting and has published patterns in a variety of quilt magazines. This is her first (but probably not her last) book.

Metric Conversion Chart

TO CONVERT	TO	MULTIPLY BY
Inches	Centimeters	2.54
Centimeters	Inches	0.4
Feet	Centimeters	30.5
Centimeters	Feet	0.03
Yards	Meters	0.9
Meters	Yards	1.1

Acknowledgements

*M*y sincerest thanks to the original Spiromaniacs who ventured into uncharted quilting territory, endured spinning brains and sleepless nights, and spent many hours at their sewing machines to create the beautiful works in this book. I could not have done this without you.

- Anita Mester, *Austin, TX*
- Barb Porter, *Lowell, MI*
- Barbara Appelbaum *New York, NY*
- Barbara Baker, *Meadow Vista, CA*
- Barbara Jones, *Norristown, PA*
- Becky Bozic, *Morgantown, WV*
- Beth Bigler, *Lancaster, PA*
- Betty Donahue, *Talladega, AL*
- Bev Anderson, *Lowell, MI*
- Caroline Anstey, *Winnisquam, NH*
- Charlotte Hill, *Delhi, NY*
- Crystal Marie, *Weaverville, CA*
- Dana Jones, *White Plains, NY*
- Devi Lanphere, *Antioch, CA*
- Dottie Lankard, *Independence, KS*
- Emma Krenek, *Manchaca, TX*
- Evelyn Larrison, *DeForest, WI*
- Fee Bricknell, *Manado, North Sulawesi, Indonesia*
- Gail Wiebe, *Carberry, Manitoba, Canada*
- Helen King, *Dumas, TX*
- Jamie McClenaghan, *Fairfield, CA*
- Jill Kerekes, *Flemington, NJ*
- Joan Garland, *Braselton, GA*

- John Flynn, *Billings, MT*
- Julie Willis, *Mesic, NC*
- Kathy Edwards, *Alexandria, VA*
- Kathy Oppelt, *Braselton, GA*
- Katie Fields, *Lenore, ID*
- Kelly Hendrickson, *Rogers, MN*
- Laurie Nathan, *New York, NY*
- Linda Cooper, *Burke, VA*
- Lois Hicks, *Kemmerer, WY*
- Marian Murdoch, *Sedbury, Chepstow, Wales*
- Mary Farr, *Gilford, NH*
- Mary Reddington, *Springfield, VA*
- Mary Ann Olmstead, *Beloit, WI*
- Micki Wiersma, *Raleigh, NC*
- Muriel Roberts, *Sheffield, England*
- Rhona Triggs, *New York, NY*
- Rhonda Adams, *Alexandria, VA*
- Robin Armstead, *Copperas Cove, TX*
- Roxanne Bowling, *Dumas, TX*
- Sandra Mettler, *Buerglen, Switzerland*
- Sandy Weber, *Alanson, MI*
- Sheila Mote, *Calgary, Alberta, Canada*
- Sheila Piasecki, *Fayetteville, NC*
- Susan Harmon, *Cherryvale, KS*

- Susan Lock, *Calgary, Alberta, Canada*
- Susanne Schmid, *Oberbussnang, Switzerland*
- Valerie Yeaton, *Oakland, CA*
- Vicki Herrman, *Knoxville, IA*

To Diana Mancini and Billy Alper at Blank Quilting, who stumbled me into the world of professional quilting when I barely knew one existed.

To the people at Krause who believed in this and helped make it happen.

To the staff of City Quilter, who never complain when I pull dozens of bolts of fabric from the shelves, particularly Nancy Rabatin who always finds the right color, even when I think it's wrong.

To Andrea at Electric Quilt for her assistance in writing and editing instructions for EQ.

And to Annette S., Lila, Trevor and Daniel, who provided constant encouragement and support, and sometimes even a sewing machine!

Dedication

*T*o my Grandmothers, who made the quilts I slept under as a child, especially to Grandma Hussey, whose quilting legacy passed to me.

And to my mother, who inadvertently made me think about doing a book in the first place.

Contents

How to Use This Book   6

Chapter 1
Meet the Spirals   8
- Shapes for Spirals
- Parts of a Spiral
- How to Draw a Nesting Spiral
- How to Draw a Baravelle Spiral
- How to Draw a Pinwheel Spiral
- How to Draw a Point-to-Point Spiral

Chapter 2
Designing With Spirals   28
- Smooth Spokes
- Spoke Variations
- Rings
- Ring Variations
- Break the Rules!
- Changing Spin Direction
- Varying the Increment
- Pinwheel With Sawtooth Edges
- Connecting Spirals
- Ribbons
- Connecting Pinwheel and Point-to-Point Spirals
- Connecting Nesting and Baravelle Spirals
- Double-Width Connections
- Bar Joins
- Centers and Surrounding Elements
- Corners
- Surrounds and Backgrounds
- Single Setting
- Free Setting
- Free Setting Using Appliqué
- Flow-Setting
- Block-as-Quilt Setting
- Mandalas
- Spirals Within Spirals
- Spiral Borders
- Choosing Colors and Fabrics
- More Choosing Colors and Fabrics
- Placing Colors and Values in a Spiral
- Fabrics that Blend
- Fabrics that Separate

- A Few More Fabric Considerations
- Gradation of Size
- Gradation of Color and Value
- Directional and Radial Fabrics
- Color Charts

Chapter 3
Sewing Spirals   80
- Preparing Foundations
- Start With the Right Materials
- Making a Spiral Foundation
- Foundation Choices
- Calculating Yardage
- Cutting Fabric for Spirals
- Preparing the Sewing Machine
- Positioning, Pinning and Taping
- Stitching Techniques
- Trimming and Pressing Seams
- Sewing Nesting and Baravelle Spirals
- Sewing Pinwheel and Point-to-Point Spirals
- Fixing Mistakes
- Joining Blocks
- Finishing the Quilt Top

Chapter 4
Projects   106
- Project 1: Spiraling Roses on My Table
  Nesting Spirals, Level: Beginner

- Project 2: Exploding Spiral
  Point-to-Point Spiral, Level: Intermediate

- Project 3: The Court Jester
  *Point-to-Point Spirals combined with other blocks,
  Level: Intermediate*

- Project 4: Zowie! Powie!
  Point-to-Point Spirals, Level: Advanced

- Project 5: Synergy
  Baravelle Spirals, Level: Advanced

Gallery of In-Spiralling Quilts   128
Appendix 1: Resources   145
Appendix 2: Yardage Calculation Chart   146
Appendix 3: Template Library   148
Index   157

The goal of this book is to inspire you to be creative in new and exciting ways. I want to give you ideas and tools, then teach you how to use them to create your own unique spiral quilts.

What's in the Book
There are three ways to use this book to make a spiral quilt:
- Make one of the projects designed for you in the Projects chapter (page 106).
- Create your own spiral quilt using templates in the *Template Library* (in the appendix and also on the accompanying CD) as building blocks.
- Design a completely original spiral quilt, applying spiral techniques in your own way.

The techniques in this book are arranged sequentially: first, the basic techniques; second, then how to put them to use; and third, how to vary them in creative ways. If you want to stick to the basics, you can skip past the variations to another page. That way, you won't get bogged down in too much information too soon. Just come back and explore the variations when you're ready. Once you get into the process of creating your spiral quilt, you'll likely find yourself using the book like a manual, jumping around from topic to topic.

Often you'll see sidebars telling you where to look for pictures of quilts on other pages. Take a moment to look at these quilts; you'll find many inspiring examples of spiral techniques and concepts.

Of course, sometimes you'll want to just browse through and enjoy looking at the simply amazing spiral quilts. Check them out on the blog as well (read on).

Online Resources

Think of this book as a door to the world of spiral quilts. To enrich the resources available and to make learning easier, the book is linked to two online resources:

- The Spiromaniacs Blog, http://spiromaniacs.wordpress. com. "How did they do that?"

Do you ever find yourself asking that question when you look at a quilt? Throughout the book, look for this symbol — 🌀 — in the captions of the quilts. Whenever it appears, it means you can find that quilt on the Spiromaniacs Blog. Once you're there, just click on the quilter's name in the Work-in-Progress Pages to see her progress from idea to finished quilt. You can also join the fun and participate in the Spiromaniacs Blog. There you can meet other spiral quilters online,

share inspiration and ideas, ask questions, solve problems and get encouragement. Be sure to sign up for the free Spiromaniacs newsletter.

- My website is also a great resource: www.ranaemerrillquilts.com. Here, you can receive free quilt patterns, sign up for newsletters and get more information on workshops and retreats.

Peeking Spirals
28" × 28"
Designed, pieced and quilted by Betty Donahue

Meet the Spirals

There are four types of spirals in this book: Nesting spirals, Baravelle spirals, Pinwheel spirals and Point-to-Point spirals. They are more similar than different, but each has its own proportions and special characteristics. In this chapter, I'll introduce you to each type, and teach you how to draw them. Take time to stop and draw the spirals as you read. Even if you plan to use the templates in the book or on the CD, drawing the spirals will help you understand how they work. Don't worry—spirals are easy to draw! All you need is a straightedge or a ruler and a pencil or erasable pen. If you tremble in terror at the mere thought of a number, take heart: Spirals do not require math!

(Electric Quilt-users, see *Drawing Spirals in Electric Quilt* on the accompanying CD.)

Shapes for Spirals

The outside edge of a spiral is its *shape*. A shape that has all sides the same length is *equilateral* ("equi" means equal and "lateral" means side). A shape that does not have all sides the same length but can be folded equally in half is *symmetrical*. A shape that has all different sides and corners is *irregular*. Most of the time, rather than using the Greek names of shapes (like "hexagon" for six sides or "dodecagon" for twelve sides), I'll refer to shapes simply by their number of sides and type: "a six-sided equilateral shape," or "a twelve-sided irregular shape."

You can draw a spiral in any shape as long as all its corners point outward—also known as a *convex polygon*.

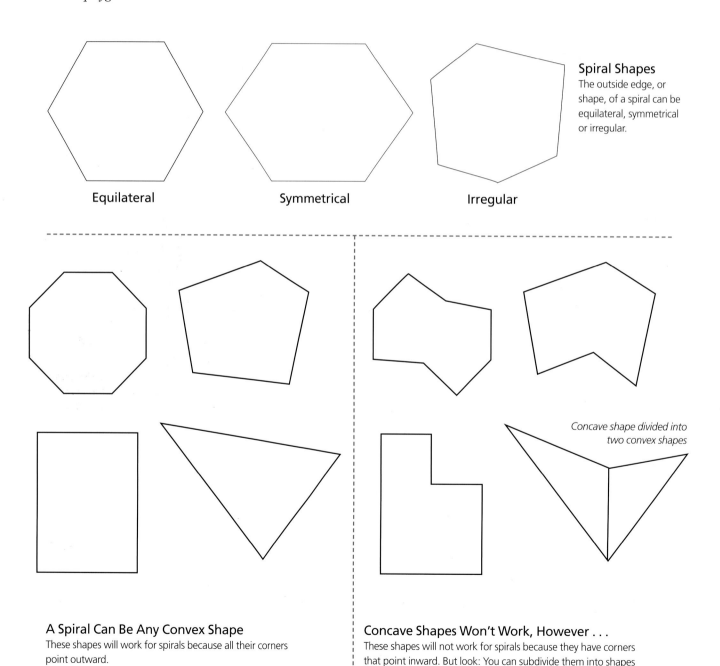

Equilateral   Symmetrical   Irregular

Spiral Shapes
The outside edge, or shape, of a spiral can be equilateral, symmetrical or irregular.

Concave shape divided into two convex shapes

A Spiral Can Be Any Convex Shape
These shapes will work for spirals because all their corners point outward.

Concave Shapes Won't Work, However . . .
These shapes will not work for spirals because they have corners that point inward. But look: You can subdivide them into shapes that do work.

Parts of a Spiral

*L*et's begin with the basic parts of a spiral and the words we'll use to talk about them.

The basic parts of a spiral are:

- *Triangles.* The basic building block of the spiral.
- *Center.* The shape in the middle around which the rings of triangles are placed.
- *Rings.* When you draw a spiral, you start at the edge of the shape and create rings of triangles going inward (toward the center). When you sew a spiral, you start at the center and sew rings of triangles outward (toward the edge).
- *Spokes.* These are the arms of the spiral made up of adjacent triangles. Contrasting fabric choices bring the spokes out.

All About Triangles

- *Base:* The side of a triangle nearest the center.
- *Peak:* The triangle's highest point, across from the base.
- *Tip:* The narrowest corner of the triangle.
- *Height:* The distance from the base to the peak.
- *Type A Triangle:* When the corner angle of a shape is 90 degrees (a right angle) or wider, the base is the longest side of the triangle, and the length of a triangle is the same as the base.
- *Type B Triangle:* When the corner angle of a shape is less than 90 degrees (as in a triangle), the peak extends beyond the base and the length of the triangle extends as far out as the peak.
- *Increment (applies to Nesting and Pinwheel spirals only):* The length of the shortest side of the triangle.
- *Primary direction of spin:* Either counterclockwise or clockwise, whichever forms a smooth spoke.

Now gather paper, pencil and straightedge, and let's draw some spirals!

Triangles

Center

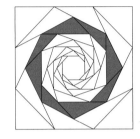

Rings

Spokes

Parts of a Spiral
A spiral is built from a center shape with rings of triangles around it. The spokes are a visual effect you create by using contrasting fabrics in the right places.

Triangle Types

The triangle type (A or B) makes a difference when you want to cut the base on the straight grain of fabric and when positioning fabric on the foundation.

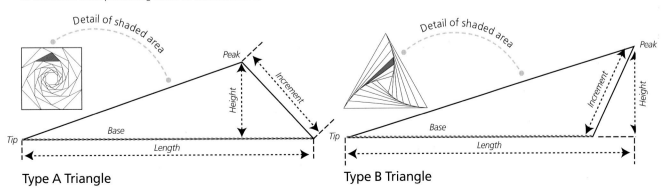

Type A Triangle

Type B Triangle

How to Draw a Nesting Spiral

I call these Nesting spirals because they remind me of those Russian nesting dolls. Nesting spirals work in any shape, though for shapes with more than eight sides the triangles become quite narrow. You may recognize the Nesting spiral as a Twisted Log Cabin block.

A Nesting Spiral Quilt
The seven spokes in this Nesting spiral represent six days of creation, and one day of rest. The finished earth is suspended in the center.

Creation
32″ × 36″
Designed, pieced and quilted by Kelly Hendrickson

Nesting Spirals in Different Shapes
Notice how the spokes become narrower and more curved as more sides are added. Shown here are three-, four-, five-, six- and eight-sided equilateral Nesting spirals.

1 Draw a Shape for the Finished Spiral

Decide on the size and shape of your finished spiral and, using a straightedge or ruler, draw it full-sized. Remember all corners of the shape must point out.

(Electric Quilt-users, see *Drawing Spirals in Electric Quilt* on the accompanying CD.)

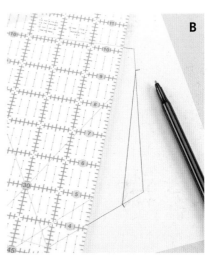

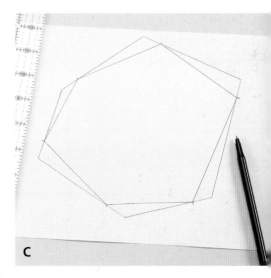

2 Mark the First Increments

Working clockwise from each corner, mark a dot between each corner and the midpoint of each side. The distance between the corner and the dot is the increment. While you are learning, a good increment is about ¾" to 1", but once you get comfortable with drawing spirals, experiment with shorter and longer increments, or with mixing them up. (See *Varying the Increment*, page 42.)

(You can also place your dots counterclockwise from the corners. Whichever direction you choose, stick with it for the entire spiral.)

3 Connect the Dots

Use the straightedge to connect dot to dot in order around the shape (figures A and B). Make sure the ends of the lines meet accurately at the dots. This forms a ring of triangles that touch at the corners and creates a new shape inside the first one with the same number of sides (figure C). (Tip: If your new shape doesn't have the same number of sides as the previous one, you either skipped a side or you mixed up the direction of the dots.)

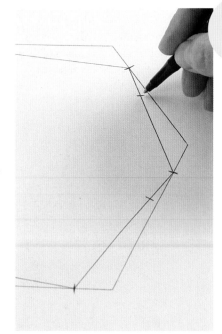

4 *Mark Dots on the New Shape*

Repeat step 2, this time on the new shape that formed inside the previous one. Mark dots in the same direction from the corner as the first set of dots. Use the same increment (distance from corner to dot) as you did in step 2.

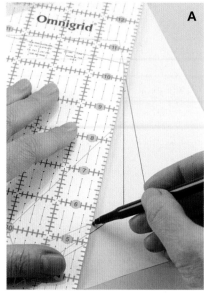

A

B

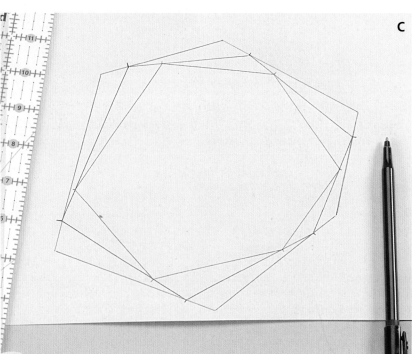

C

Characteristics of Nesting Spirals

- Nesting spirals allow you to control the height of the triangles by changing the placement of the dot (the length of the increment). For example, you may want to make triangles narrower as they approach the center to create a sense of perspective, or you may want to alternate narrower and wider triangles for a fun, freeform spiral. (See *Varying the Increment*, page 42.)

- Nesting spirals are the easiest spirals to sew. They do not require partial-seam piecing and several triangles can be sewn at a time. (See *Sewing Nesting and Baravelle Spirals*, page 94.)

- Because the triangles that form Nesting spirals do not completely cover the sides of the outside shape, they sometimes need special attention with you combine them with other spirals. (See *Connecting Spirals*, page 45–46.)

5 *Connect Dots to Form the Second Ring*

Repeat step 3, connecting the new set of dots to form the second ring (figures A, B and C). You may find it helpful to draw this second ring of triangles in a different color.

6 Continue Adding Rings

After several repetitions of steps 2 and 3, you will see the spokes of the spiral being formed by the adjacent triangles in successive rings.

**Good Gracious
Great Ball of Fire!**
page 140

Nesting Spiral Quilts in This Book

- Bev, Barb & A Bottle of Wine *page 142*
- Creation *page 12*
- Dark Star/Spiral of Life *page 60*
- Flying Tumbleweeds *page 57*
- Good Gracious Great Ball of Fire! *page 138*
- Hot & Cold *page 59*
- Jade Crystals *page 37*
- Mesclun Mixed *page 45*
- Midsummer (also Point-to-Point) *page 64*
- Northern Stars *page 36*
- Oriental Fantasy *page 66*

- Purple Spiral #1 (Down the Drain) *page 20*
- Ribbons of Life (also Pinwheel) *page 62*
- Roses Are My Best Friends *page 57*
- Spiraling Roses on My Table *page 108*
- Splish Splash Spirals *page 134*
- Sustenance *page 58*
- Untitled (Red, White & Black) *page 58*
- We're Not In Kansas Anymore! (also Point-to-Point) *page 137*
- Whirlygig *page 141*

How to Draw a Baravelle Spiral

*B*aravelle spirals are the "twirliest" of the spiral types. They are formed by dividing each side of the shape in half, then connecting the halfway points to draw a new shape inside the first one. Baravelle spirals are named for James Baravelle (BEAR-a-vell), the eighteenth-century mathematician who discovered them. Baravelle spirals work in any shape. You may recognize the square Baravelle spiral as a traditional Snail's Trail block.

A Baravelle Spiral Quilt
This wonderful quilt uses six-sided Baravelle spirals with rainbow color-to-color gradation. (See *Gradation of Color and Value*, page 76.)

Big Bang + One Second
60" × 80"
Designed, pieced and quilted by John Flynn

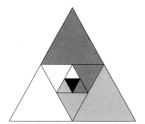 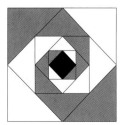   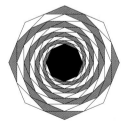

Baravelle Spirals in Different Shapes
Shown here are three-, four-, five-, six- and eight-sided equilateral Baravelle spirals.

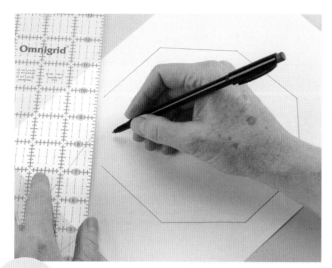

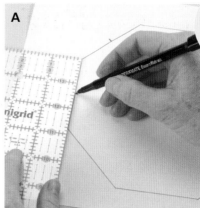

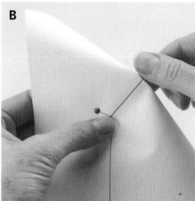

1 Draw a Shape for the Finished Spiral

Decide on the size and shape of your finished spiral and using a straightedge or ruler, draw it full-sized. Remember that all corners must point out.

(Electric Quilt-users, see *Drawing Spirals in Electric Quilt* on the accompanying CD.)

2 Mark the Midpoint of Each Side

On each side of the shape, mark a dot at the exact center of the side, so it is divided in half. You can measure this with a ruler (figure A) or fold the line in half to determine the center point of the side (figure B). Use a pin to match the ends of the line.

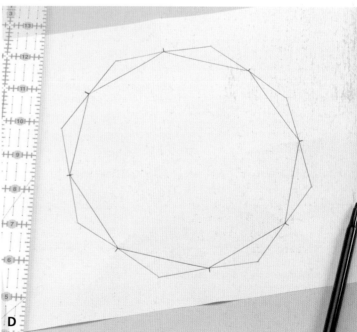

3 Connect the Dots

Use the straightedge to connect dot to dot in order around the shape (figure C). Make sure the ends of the lines meet accurately on the dots. This forms a ring of triangles that touch at the corners and creates a new shape inside the first one with the same number of sides (figure D). (Tip: If your new shape doesn't have the same number of sides as the previous one, you skipped a side.)

4 *Mark Dots on the New Shape*

Repeat step 2, this time on the midpoints of the sides of the new shape that formed inside the previous one.

Characteristics of Baravelle Spirals

- Baravelle spirals and Nesting spirals (on the previous page) are "first cousins"—they are both drawn "dot-to-dot" around the shape. The difference is Baravelle spirals always have the dot at the center of the side while Nesting spirals' dots are off-center.

- The proportions of a Baravelle spiral are set using the midpoint of each side to draw them, so you cannot vary the triangles within the spiral.

- Baravelle spirals spin equally in both directions within the spiral, so you can create double spirals and interlocking spokes like the ones in the quilt on this book's cover. (See *Spoke Variations*, page 32.) They can also be colored to create many non-spiral designs such as snowflakes and pineapples. (See *Rings* on page 34.)

- Baravelle spirals are sewn in the same way as Nesting spirals—they do not require partial-seam piecing and can be sewn several triangles at a time. (See *Sewing, Nesting and Baravelle Spirals*, page 94.)

- Baravelle spirals can have many small pieces, but since several triangles can be sewn at a time, they can actually be sewn quickly.

- Because the triangles that form Baravelle spirals do not completely cover the sides of the outside shape, they usually require sashing to combine with other spirals. (See *Connecting Spirals*, page 45–46.)

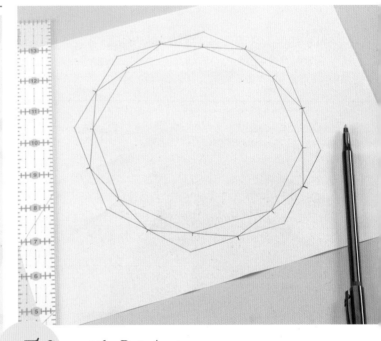

5 *Connect the Dots Again*

Repeat step 3, connecting the new set of dots to form a second ring.

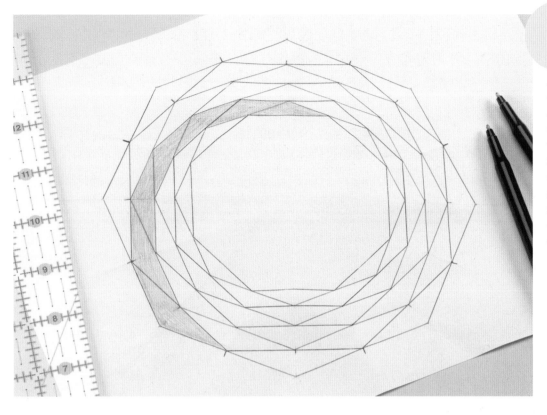

6 Continue Adding Rings

After several repetitions of steps 2 and 3, you will see the spokes of the spiral being formed by the adjacent triangles in successive rings. The spokes can spin in either direction.

Crop Circles: How'd They Do That?
page 137

Baravelle Spiral Quilts in This Book

- Big Bang + One Second *page 16*

- Crop Circles: How'd They Do That? *page 135*

- Ellen's Star Rising (also uses Pinwheel spirals), *page 139*

- Enjoy the Journey *page 132*

- Midwinter (also uses Point-to-Point spirals) *page 65*

- My Bloomin' Spiral *page 56*

- Over the Rainbow *page 132*

- Peeking Spirals (also uses Point-to-Point spirals) *pages 8, 39*

- Plum Crazy *page 53*

- Spiral of Life *page 131*

- Synergy, *page 124*

- Tree Canopy *page 38*

- Vestments for St. Bart's *page 67*

- Whirlpool Galaxy: A Glorious Creation *page 71*

How to Draw a Pinwheel Spiral

I call these Pinwheel spirals because the triangles interlock in a way that reminds me of a pinwheel. Pinwheel spirals are very similar to Nesting spirals, but as you learn more about them you'll find they can do some things Nesting spirals can't. Like Nesting spirals, Pinwheel spirals work in any shape, though for shapes with more than eight sides the triangles become quite narrow. And like Nesting spirals, you may recognize Pinwheel spirals as another variation on the Twisted Log Cabin block.

A Pinwheel Spiral Quilt
The center of this quilt is an eight-sided Pinwheel spiral and the corners are mirrored pairs of triangle Pinwheel spirals.

Purple Spiral #1 (Down the Drain)
27" × 27"
Designed, pieced and quilted by Valerie Yeaton

 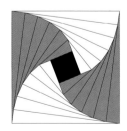   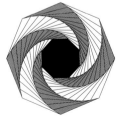

Pinwheel Spirals in Different Shapes
Shown here are three-, four-, five-, six- and eight-sided equilateral Pinwheel spirals.

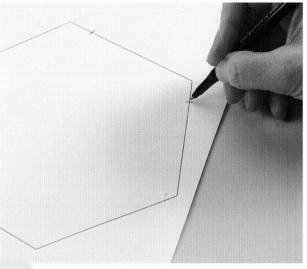

1 *Draw a Shape for the Spiral*

Decide on the size and shape of your finished spiral and, using a straightedge or ruler, draw it full-sized. Remember all the corners must point out.

(Electric Quilt-users, see *Drawing Spirals in Electric Quilt* on the accompanying CD.)

2 *Mark the First Increments*

Working clockwise from each corner, mark a dot between each corner and the midpoint of each side. The distance between the corner and the dot is the increment. While you are learning, a good increment is about ¾" to 1", but once you get comfortable with drawing spirals, experiment with shorter and longer increments, or with mixing them up. (See *Varying the Increments*, page 42.)

(You can also place your dots counterclockwise from the corners. Whichever direction you choose, stick with it for the entire spiral.)

3 *Connect Corners to Dots*

Connect the first dot to a corner of the shape like this: Put the index finger of one hand on a dot, then with the other hand, start at the dot, trace counterclockwise around the edge of the shape and stop at the second corner you come to. Use the straightedge to draw a line between this corner and the dot where you started (A, B). Make sure the ends of the lines meet the corner and the dot precisely. Repeat for each dot, working in order around the shape. It helps to turn the paper as you work. As you work around the shape, the new lines will cross the tips of the triangles before them.

(If you marked the dots *counterclockwise* from the corners, circle *clockwise*.)

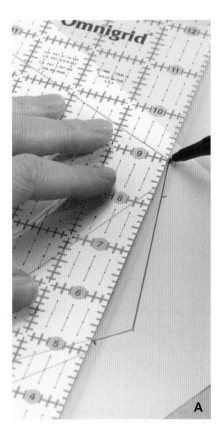

A

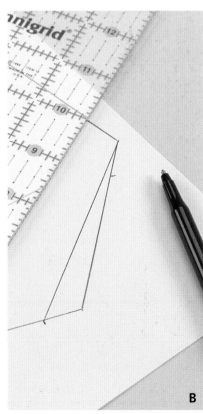

B

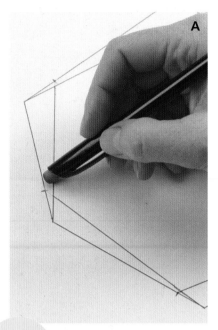

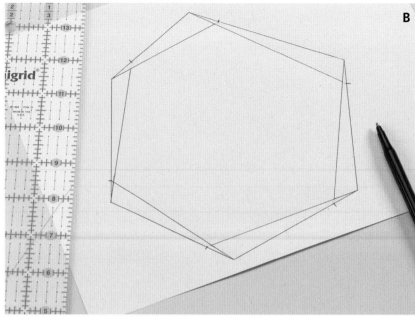

4 *Erase the Unneeded Lines*

Erase the short bits of line that cross the tip of each triangle (A). (When you get more comfortable drawing Pinwheel spirals, you can end each line where it meets the previous line, so you won't have to go back and erase the crossovers.)

When you're done (B), you'll see a ring of triangles with the short side of each triangle laying against a long side of the triangle next to it, and a new shape inside the previous one, with the same number of sides.

Characteristics of Pinwheel Spirals

- The proportions of Pinwheel spirals are almost identical to Nesting spirals.

- The triangles that form Pinwheel spirals completely cover the sides of the outside shape, so Pinwheel spirals combine smoothly with other Pinwheel or Point-to-Point spirals. This can make a big difference in the look of your overall design. (See *Connecting Spirals*, pages 45–46.)

- Like Nesting spirals, Pinwheel spirals allow you to control the height of the triangles. (See *Varying the Increments*, page 42.)

- In Pinwheel spirals the short side of each triangle lies against the long side of the next triangle in the ring. This makes for the possibility of continuous rings of color in a Pinwheel spiral. (See *Rings*, page 34.)

- Pinwheel spirals must be sewn one triangle at a time and usually require partial-seam piecing. (See *Sewing Pinwheel and Point-to-Point Spirals*, page 96.)

- Pinwheel spirals are the only type of spiral that will create sawtooth edges. (See *Sawtooth Edges*, pages 44, 99.)

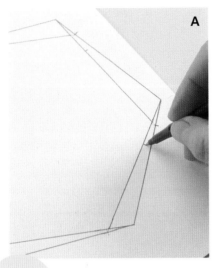

A

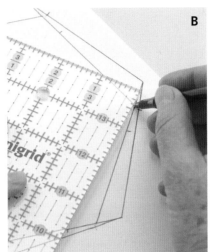

B

Pinwheel Spiral Quilts in This Book

- Brightly Churned *page 51*
- Do You See? *page 144*
- Ellen's Star Rising (also uses Baravelle spirals) *page 139*
- Florida 2007 *shown below, page 44*
- Hearts Form From Pieces *page 62*
- Majestic Mandalai - A Personal Journey *page 140*
- Not My Dad's Bow Ties *page 61*
- Purple Spiral #1 (Down the Drain) *pages 20, 28*
- Ribbons of Life (also uses Nesting spirals) *page 62*
- Sails & Waves *page 136*
- Spiro Pony From Texas *page 58*
- We've Got Sisters! *page 100*

5 Repeat to Form a Second Ring of Triangles

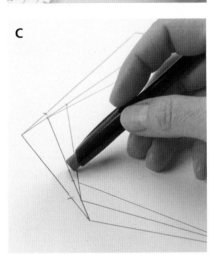

C

Working inside the new shape, repeat the process of marking dots (A), connecting dots to corners (B), and erasing unneeded lines (C) to form a second ring of triangles. Work in the same direction from the corner as you did for the first set of dots. You may find it helpful to use a different color for each new ring of triangles.

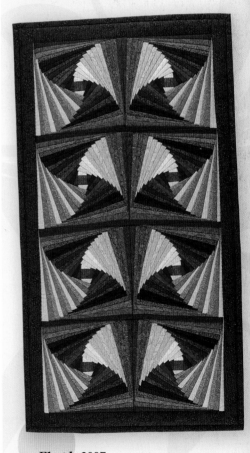

Florida 2007
page 44

6 Repeat for More Rings

Keep repeating steps 2, 3 and 4, each time working inside the new ring you just formed. After several repetitions you will see the spokes of the spiral being formed by the adjacent triangles in successive rings.

How to Draw a Point-to-Point Spiral

*P*oint-to-Point spirals are drawn by connecting the corners of the outside shape. Point-to-Point spirals only work in shapes with five or more sides. There are two methods for drawing Point-to-Point spirals. Step 1, setting up the outside shape, is the same for both. After that, try Method A and Method B to see which works better for you.

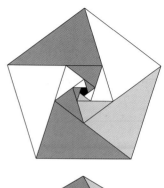

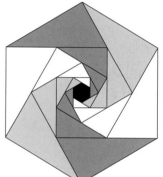

A Point-to-Point Spiral Quilt
This eight-sided Point-to-Point spiral was the first spiral quilt I ever made—just to see if the idea really worked. Apparently, it did! Bias tape accents the edges of the spokes. Notice the careful placement of the stripes (see *Directional and Radial Fabrics*, page 78).

Holiday Whirl
45" × 54"
Designed, pieced and quilted by RaNae Merrill

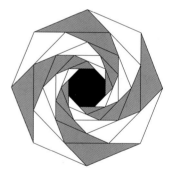

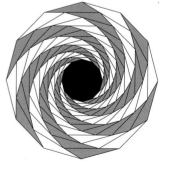

Point-to-Point Spirals in Different Shapes
Shown here are five-, six-, eight- and twelve-sided equilateral Point-to-Point spirals.

Point-to-Point Spiral, Method A

1 Draw the Outer Shape

Decide on the size and shape of your finished spiral and, using a straightedge or ruler, draw it full-sized. Remember all corners must point out.

(Electric Quilt-users, see *Drawing Spirals in Electric Quilt* on the accompanying CD.)

2 Connect Corners to Form the First Triangle

Choose any corner of the shape and call it the first corner. Working in either direction, draw a line connecting the first corner to the third. Make sure the ends of the lines meet precisely at the corners.

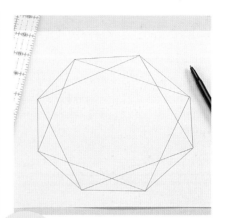

3 Connect the Remaining Corners

Working in the same direction, continue to draw lines to connect every other corner until you arrive back where you started. If the shape has an uneven number of sides, one trip around the shape will connect all the corners. (If you've ever drawn a five-pointed star by drawing criss-cross from point to point, you've already done this.) If the shape has an even number of sides, one trip around the shape will connect half the corners, so start at an empty corner and repeat this step to connect the rest.

4 Erase Unneeded Lines

Every corner of the outer shape now has two lines that extend inward from the corner and cross a line. Erase one of these two lines from the corner to where it crosses another line. Choose either the lines on the clockwise side or on the counterclockwise side—which side you choose determines which direction the spiral turns. (Choose the same side in all rings of the spiral.) As you erase, a ring of triangles appears with the short side of each triangle adjoining the long side of the triangle next to it.

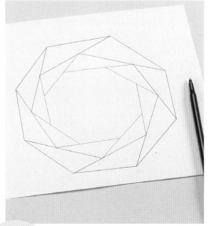

5 Draw More Rings

Repeat steps 2 through 4 several times, each time in the new shape that forms inside the previous one. You may find it helpful to use a different color to draw each new ring of triangles. After several repetitions you will see the spokes of the spiral formed by the adjacent triangles in successive rings.

Point-to-Point Spiral, Method B

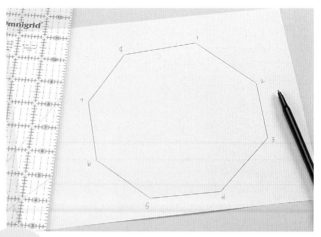

1 Draw the Outer Shape
Decide on the size and shape of your finished spiral and, using a straightedge or ruler, draw it full-sized. Remember all corners must point out.

2 Number the Corners
Number the corners of the shape in order clockwise around the outer edge. (To reverse the direction of the spin, number the corners counterclockwise.)

Characteristics of Point-to-Point Spirals

- The proportions of a Point-to-Point spiral are set by using the corners of the shape to draw them, so you cannot vary the triangles.

- In a Point-to-Point spiral the short sides of the triangles adjoin the long sides of the adjacent triangles (like a Pinwheel spiral), so you can color the rings in continuous bands of color. (See *Rings*, page 34.)

- The sides of Point-to-Points are completely covered by a single triangle (like Pinwheel spirals), so they connect smoothly with other Point-to-Point and Pinwheel spirals in flow settings. (See *Connecting Spirals*, pages 45–46.)

- Point-to-Point spirals must be sewn one triangle at a time and usually require partial-seam piecing. (See *Sewing Pinwheel and Point-to-Point Spirals*, page 96.)

A

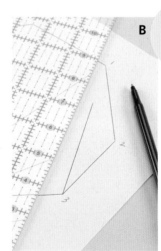

B

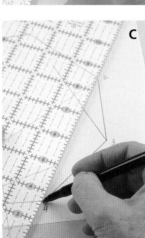

C

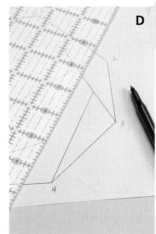

D

3 Draw the First Line
Align your ruler with corners #1 and #3. Starting at corner #3, draw a line toward corner #1, stopping about three-quarters of the distance to corner #1.

4 Draw the Second Line
Align your ruler with corners #2 and #4 (C). Starting at corner #4, draw a line toward corner #2, stopping where it meets the line you just drew (D).

Point-to-Point Spiral Quilts in This Book

- City Tears to Country Smiles
  page 130

- Exploding Spiral
  shown below and page 112

- Grandpa Shirts *page 40*

- Holiday Whirl *page 24*

- In Memory of Marja *page 133*

- Infinite Rainbow *page 128*

- Midsummer (also uses Nesting spirals) *page 64*

- Midwinter (also uses Baravelle spirals) *page 65*

- Peeking Spirals (also uses Baravelle spirals)
  pages 8, 39

- Photo Op?! *page 129*

- Spiral Frame *page 52*

- Spiral Pansies *page 35*

- Starry Night *page 69*

- Tannenbaum Twist (also uses Nesting spirals) *page 115*

- The Court Jester *page 118*

- Vroom! Vroom! *page 55*

- We're Not In Kansas Anymore! (also uses Nesting spirals) *page 137*

- Winged Water *page 33*

- Zowie! Powie! *page 120*

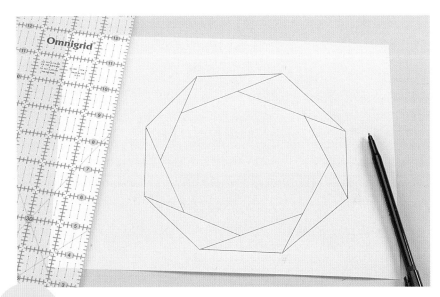

5 *Finish the First Ring*

Repeat step 4 for corners #3 and #5, corners #4 and #6, etc., drawing the line from the higher numbered corner toward the lower numbered corner, until you arrive back at the first triangle. (The next-to-last line will go from corner #1 toward the next to last number, and the last line will go from corner #2 toward the last number.) Close up the space between the end of the first line and the last line (or erase the first line if it overlaps). As you draw lines, a ring of triangles appears with the short side of each triangle adjoining the long side of the triangle next to it.

6 *Draw More Rings*

Repeat steps 2 through 5 several times, each time in the new shape that forms inside the previous one. You may find it helpful to use a different color to draw each new ring of triangles. After several repetitions you will see the spokes of the spiral formed by the adjacent triangles in successive rings.

Exploding Spiral
page 112

Purple Spiral #1 (Down the Drain)
27" × 27"
Designed, pieced and quilted by Valerie Yeaton

Designing With Spirals

*I*n this chapter, you'll also learn how to incorporate spirals into a quilt design. Keep paper, pencil and ruler handy to draw while you read. As you explore the concepts presented here, choose the forms and techniques that appeal to you and develop them into your own design. First, you'll see how to color single spirals in creative ways. Next, you'll learn how to connect and combine spirals. Finally, you'll explore ways to lay out a whole spiral quilt design, including what will go in and around the spirals: the centers, corners, backgrounds and borders. These elements can be as important as the spirals in your design. When you feel ready, go all out and combine spirals with other techniques, such as other blocks, appliqué or ornamentation.

The quilts on the following pages will show you how other quilters have used spirals in their own unique quilt designs.

There's lots to learn in this chapter. Let's get started!

Smooth Spokes

The most basic design within a spiral is its smooth spokes. All spirals have smooth spokes in the primary direction of spin. Baravelle spirals have smooth spokes in both directions (see *Double Spokes*, page 32).

If the shape has only a few sides, its sides are long relative to the overall shape, which makes the spokes look like petals of a flower. The more sides a shape has, the shorter the sides become, so the spokes become narrower and more like ribbons. To see this, compare the three-sided spirals with the eight-sided spirals in the chart at right.

The width of the spokes and how much they spin are also influenced by the type of spiral. Nesting and Pinwheel spirals have the least spin and the widest spokes. A Point-to-Point spiral with the same shape will have a similar amount of spin, but the spokes are less smooth. A Baravelle spiral with the same shape will have the most spin and the narrowest, smoothest spokes. To see this, compare the different types of spirals with the same number of sides in the chart at right.

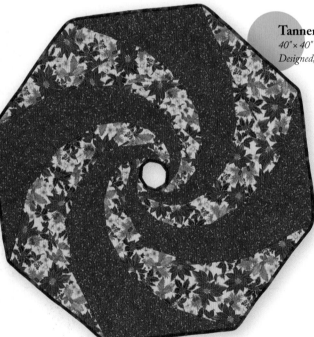

Tannenbaum Twist
40" × 40"
Designed, pieced and quilted by Beth Bigler

Spiral of Life
43½" × 43"
Designed, pieced and machine quilted by Susanne Schmid

Smooth Spokes
This Christmas tree skirt features a single Point-to-Point spiral with smooth spokes.

Smooth Spokes
This quilt features a single Baravelle spiral with smooth spokes in both directions.

Spiral Comparison Chart

This chart shows various sizes and types of spirals, with their smooth spokes indicated in gray. To make it easy to compare spirals, all the shapes in the chart are equilateral, but remember, when creating your own spirals, the sides of a spiral shape do not have to be the same length.

Number of Sides	Nesting	Pinwheel	Point-to-Point	Baravelle
3	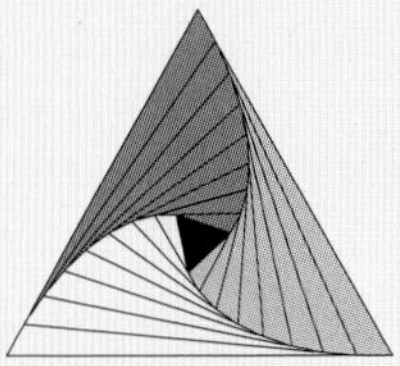	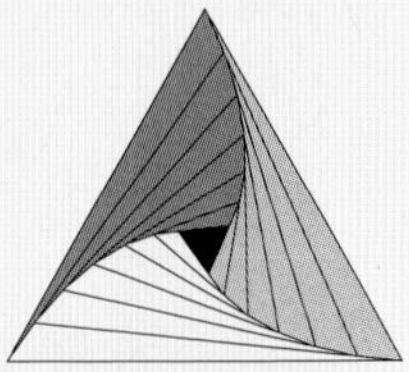	Cannot be drawn in a triangle	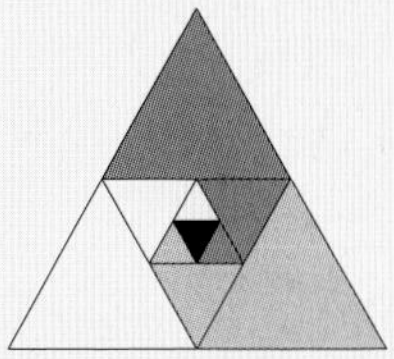
4	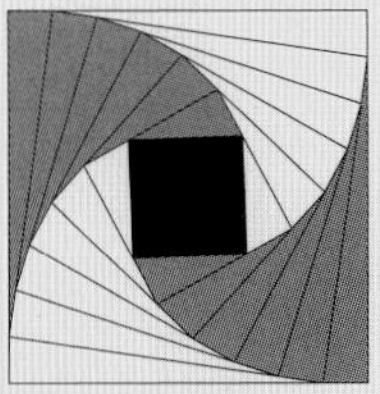	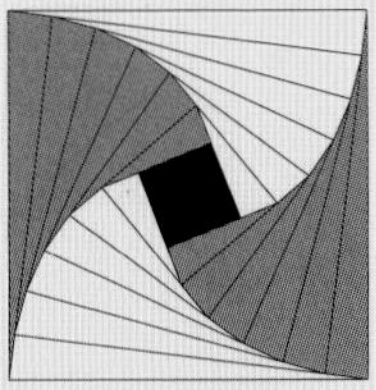	Cannot be drawn in a four-sided shape	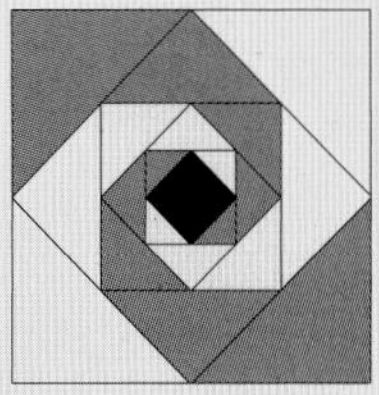
5	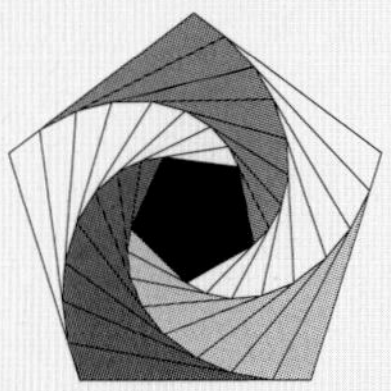	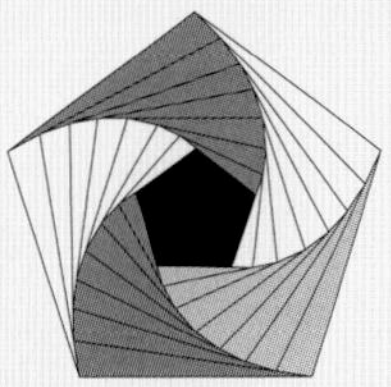	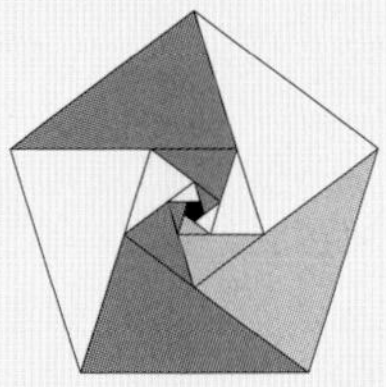	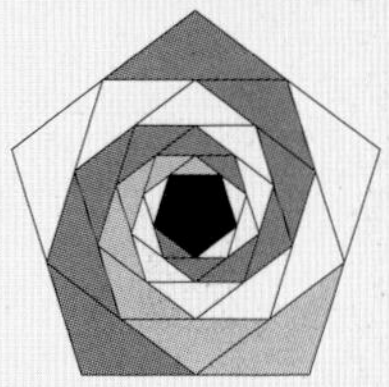
6	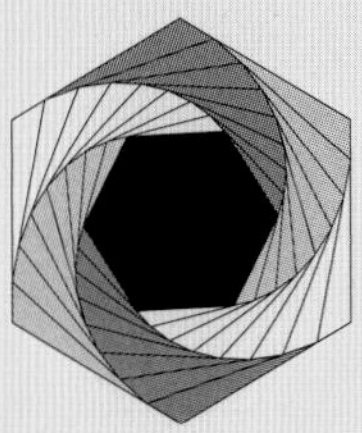	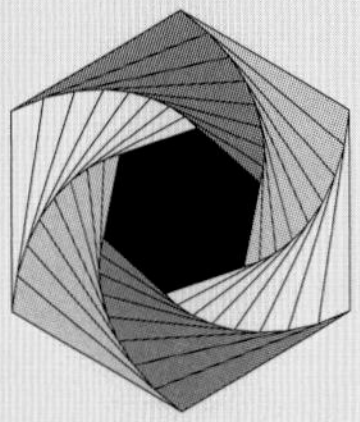	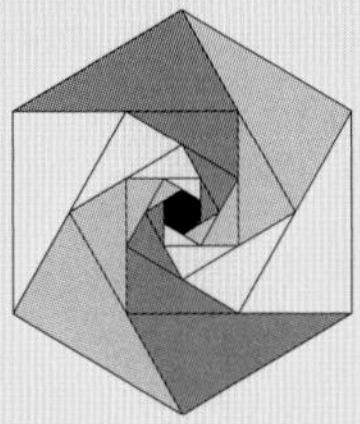	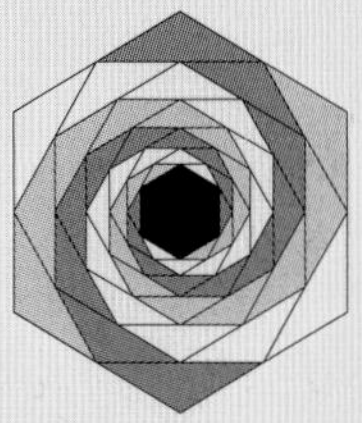
8	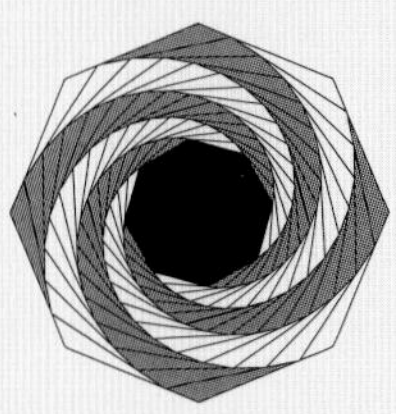	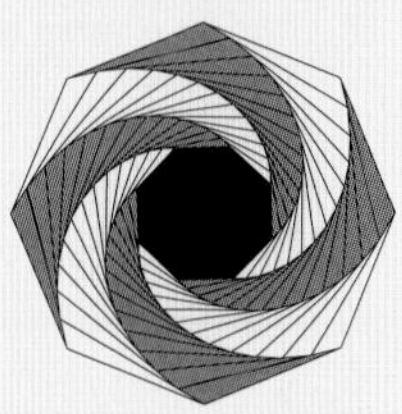	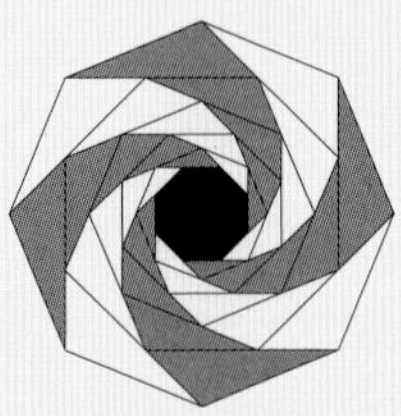	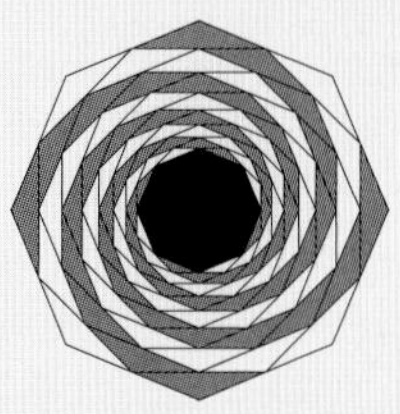
12	Triangles become too narrow unless the spiral is very large	Triangles become too narrow unless the spiral is very large	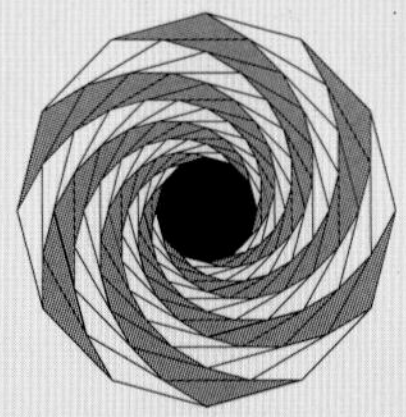	Triangles become quite small unless the spiral is very large

Spoke Variations

If you want to stick to the basics for now, skip to *Connecting Spirals* (page 45–46), then return to pages 32–44 later.

*Y*ou can create interesting designs within a spiral simply by changing color mid-spoke or by coloring in the opposite direction of the spokes.

Double Spokes (Baravelle Only)

Baravelle spirals have smooth spokes in both directions, offering the possibility of interwoven spokes. Begin at any triangle and color the triangles leading away from it in both directions.

Interrupted Spokes

Change the color abruptly in the middle of a spoke to create secondary designs. In multiple spiral settings, this can create a kaleidoscopic effect.

Quilts With Double Spokes in This Book

- Spiral of Life *page 131*
- Synergy *page 124*

Quilts With Interrupted Spokes in This Book

- Mesclun Mixed *page 45*
- Brightly Churned *page 51*

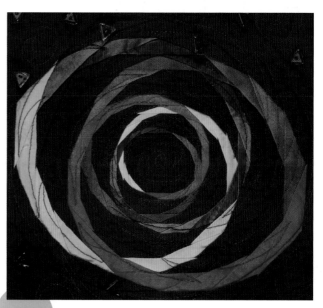

Detail, Enjoy the Journey
page 132

Double Spokes (Baravelle spirals only)
Baravelle spirals have smooth spokes in both directions, offering the possibility of interwoven spokes. Begin at any triangle and color the triangles leading away from it in both directions.

Interrupted Spokes
Change color abruptly in the middle of a spoke to create secondary designs.

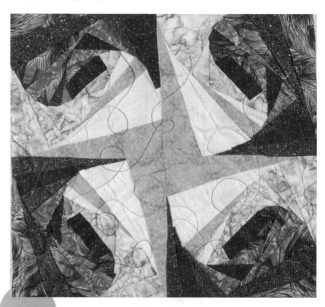

Detail, Bev, Barb & a Bottle of Wine
page 142

Multiple Interrupted Spokes
In multiple spiral settings, interrupted spokes can create a kaleidoscopic effect.

Feathered Spokes

Point-to-Point, Pinwheel and Nesting spirals have feathered spokes that appear when you color triangles in the opposite direction of the smooth spokes. Feathered spokes can be used alone or combined with smooth spokes.

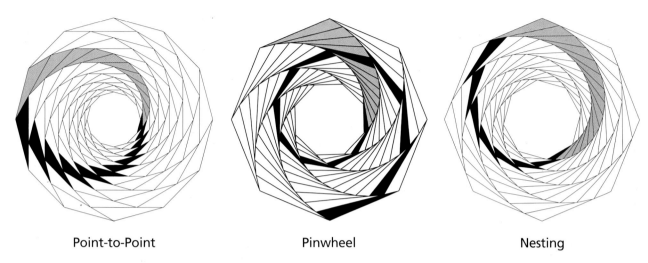

| Point-to-Point | Pinwheel | Nesting |

Feathered and Smooth Spokes Revealed

In each diagram, light gray shows the smooth spoke and black shows the feathered spoke. Point-to-Point and Pinwheel spirals: Starting with a triangle in the innermost ring of the spiral, move outward, coloring the triangle whose base touches the peak of the previous triangle. Nesting spirals: The feathered spoke skips a ring. Moving from the center outward, the peak of a triangle in the first ring touches the base of a triangle in the third ring; the peak of a triangle in the third ring touches the base of a triangle in the fifth ring, etc.

Quilts With Feathered Spokes in This Book

- Photo Op?! *page 129*
- Whirlygig *page 141*

Feathered Spokes

This sixteen-sided Point-to-Point spiral with feathered spokes was inspired by Native American baskets.

Winged Water
42½" × 51"
Designed and pieced by Susan Harmon
Machine-quilted by Cotie Campbell

Rings

*B*y now you know that spirals are built with rings of triangles. For an entirely different effect, you can color the rings instead of the spokes.

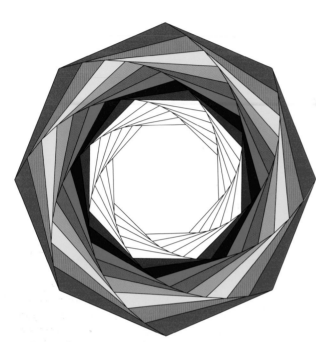

Pinwheel Spiral With Rings
Coloring the rings in a Pinwheel (or a Point-to-Point) spiral creates solid bands of color because the short side of each triangle lies against the long side of the next triangle in the ring.

Point-to-Point Spiral With Rings
Turn a Pinwheel (or a Point-to-Point) spiral into a sphere or a doughnut by arranging colored rings from dark to light.

Blue Sphere Experiment
8" diameter
Designed and sewn by Dottie Lankard

Quilts With Rings in This Book

● Dark Star/Spiral of Life *page 60*

● Enjoy the Journey *page 132*

● Flying Tumbleweeds *page 57*

● Midsummer *page 64*

● Midwinter *page 65*

● Northern Stars *page 36*

● Peeking Spirals *page 8, 39*

● Purple Spiral #1 (Down the Drain) *pages 20, 28*

Nesting Spiral With Rings
In Nesting spirals, coloring the rings creates a checkerboard effect because the sides of the triangles don't touch.

Detail, Untitled (Red, White & Black)
page 58

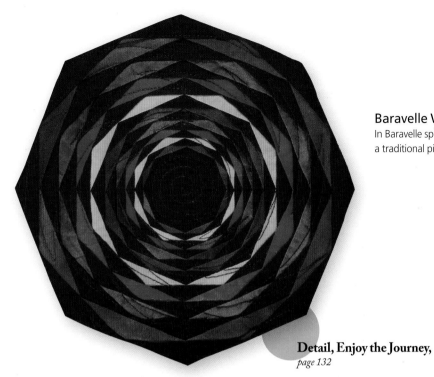

Baravelle With Rings

In Baravelle spirals, coloring the rings results in a traditional pineapple design.

Detail, Enjoy the Journey,
page 132

Ring Around the Posies

This bold design uses two different seven-sided irregular Point-to-Point spirals with colored rings.

Spiral Pansies
32" × 27"
Designed, sewn and quilted by Rhona Triggs

Ring Variations

*C*hanging the number of rings in neighboring spirals or changing colors in a ring are simple ways to add interest to a spiral design.

Varied Number of Rings

In a multiple spiral setting, introduce variety into the pattern by using some spirals with more rings than others. This entire quilt is made of the same half-square triangle block, but blocks outlined in dark purple have only one ring of triangles colored as a ring, while the purple, green and blue blocks have six rings of triangles colored as spokes.

Northern Stars
45" × 45"
Designed and pieced by Susan Lock
Quilted by Sheila Mote

Sunbursts (Point-to-Point Spirals Only)

Color an entire ring in one color, then in the next ring alternate that color with a different color in every other triangle to create the "rays" of the sun.

Detail, Midsummer *page 64*

Shards

*C*olor disconnected triangles in a spiral to create flashes of color. You might find an effective design in accenting a spiral with an occasional shard, or you may obliterate the spiral design altogether.

Crystalized Quilt
This quilt began with a half-square triangle Nesting spiral that was drawn with uneven increments. Some disconnected triangles were colored as shards. The resulting design looks like crystals.

Jade Crystals
40" × 40"
Designed, sewn and quilted by Sheila Mote

Quilts With Shards in This Book

- Do You See? *page 144*
- Enjoy the Journey *page 132*
- Over the Rainbow *page 132*
- Splish Splash Spirals *page 134*
- Starry Night *page 69*

Detail, Do You See? *page 144*

Detail, Enjoy the Journey *page 134*

Break the Rules!

Beyond Spokes or Rings

Spirals can be colored in many ways that result in designs other than spirals. Baravelle spirals are particularly versatile because their double-direction spin allows the spokes to wander.

Tree Canopy
12" × 15"
Designed, sewn and quilted by Marian Murdoch

Wandering Lines

This quilter was inspired by a drive through a canopy of trees over a road in the Welsh countryside. Although she began with a Baravelle spiral, she wandered outside the line of the spokes. (Let's hope she's more careful about the lanes on the road!)

A Spiral Quilt That Breaks the Rules

- Spiro Pony From Texas *page 58*

When is a Spiral Not a Spiral?

These drawings were preliminary sketches for Enjoy the Journey on page 132. Each is a Baravelle spiral colored to produce an effect that is *not* a spiral.

Partial Spirals

Instead of using a complete spiral in a design, use only a portion of one. Either piece a partial spiral, or piece a complete spiral and cut it up.

Piece Partial Spirals

The "waves" around the center of this quilt were pieced as single spokes.

Detail, Sails & Waves
page 136

Piece a Whole Spiral, Then Cut It Up

This quilt uses eight-sided equilateral Point-to-Point spirals—the center one colored in rings and the surrounding ones in spokes—for the center panel. Cut-up Baravelle spirals form the edging.

Peeking Spirals
28" × 28"
Designed, sewn and machine-quilted by Betty Donahue

Changing the Spin Direction

*I*n any type of spiral you can reverse the direction of spin in mid-spiral. The effect is different in each type of spiral, and also varies with how often you change direction.

Grandpa Shirts
44" × 44"
Designed and sewn by Barbara Appelbaum
Quilted by Joan Gamble

A Change of Direction
Barbara cut up her ex-husband's shirts after her divorce for this quilt (which was her first ever). She used Point-to-Point spirals, changing direction in each ring.

Detail, Over the Rainbow
page 132

Baravelle With Directional Change
This Baravelle spiral changes direction every fourth ring.

Quilts With Direction Changes in This Book

- Enjoy the Journey *page 132*
- Over the Rainbow *page 132*
- Zowie! Powie! *page 120*

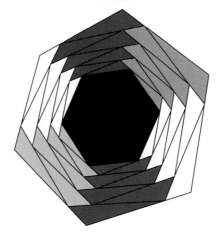

Nesting Spiral With Direction Change in Each Ring
Changing direction after each ring produces a pattern that resembles a flight of steps.

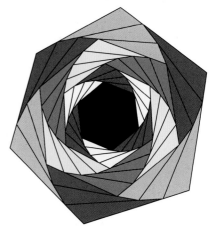

Nesting Spiral With Direction Change Every Third or Fourth Ring
The effect suggest a rose.

How to Change Direction

Changing direction in a spiral requires a couple simple changes to the way you learned to draw them in chapter 1.

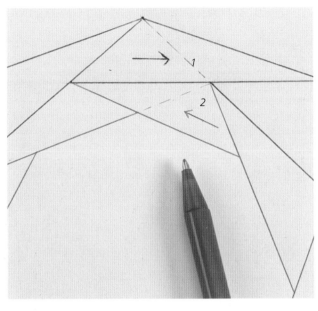

Point-to-Point Spirals: Method A

After drawing lines between all the corners of the shape, erase one of the two lines that extends in from the corner. If you were erasing the line on the right (1), then erase the line on the left (2) in the changing ring, and vice versa.

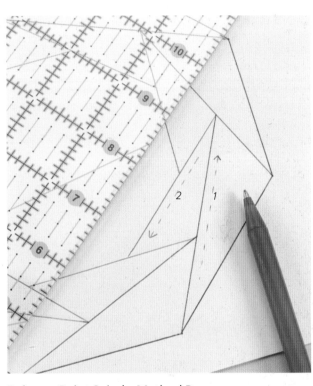

Point-to-Point Spirals: Method B

If you were drawing the line from the higher number to the lower number (1), then draw the line from the lower number to the higher number (2) in the changing ring. If you were drawing the line from the lower number to the higher number, in the changing ring draw the line from the higher number to the lower number.

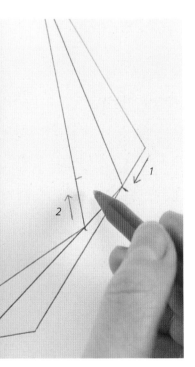

Nesting and Pinwheel Spirals

If you're marking dots clockwise from the corner (1), switch to marking them counterclockwise in the changing ring (2), and vice versa.

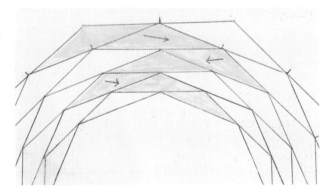

Baravelle Spirals

There is no change in the way the spiral is drawn, since Baravelle spirals spin equally in both directions, but the zigzag effect only shows up in spirals with five or more sides. To change direction, simply choose the triangle in the opposite direction from where you were headed before.

Varying the Increment

When you draw Nesting and Pinwheel spirals, you mark a dot on each side of the shape, then draw a line to that dot. Varying the distance from the corner of the shape to the dot (the increment) changes the length of the short side of the triangle and allows you to play with the proportions of the spiral. You can change the increment on different sides of the shape and/or change the increment in different rings as you draw the spiral. The possibilities for variation are limitless: Have fun playing to see what you come up with. For the sake of comparison, all the examples shown here are squares, but this will work in any shape.

Detail, Splish Splash Spirals
page 134

Perspective Variation

The basic method for drawing a Nesting or Pinwheel spiral keeps all the increments the same. Perspective variation keeps the increments the same on all sides, but progressively shrinks the increments as they move toward the center, creating a spiral with a strong sense of perspective. The sense of perspective works especially well with gradations (see *Gradation of Color and Value*, page 76). This technique can be combined with any others on this page.

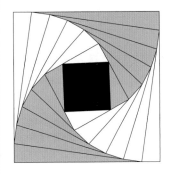 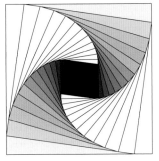

Basic Spiral   Perspective

Off-Center Nesting and Pinwheel Spirals

Draw larger increments on half the adjacent sides of the shape and smaller increments on the other adjacent sides. This variation creates an off-center spiral, pulling the center of the spiral toward the sides with shorter increments.

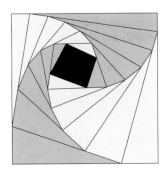 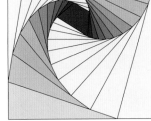

Off-Center   Off-Center + Perspective

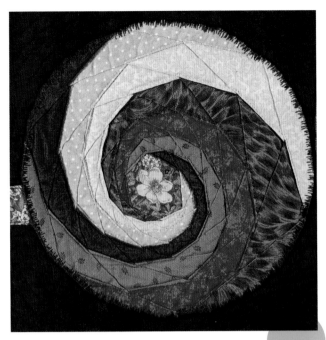

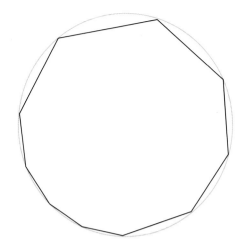

**Detail, Crop Circles:
How'd They Do That?**
page 135

Off-Center Baravelle and Point-to-Point Spirals

With Baravelle spirals or Point-to-Point spirals, the proportions of the spiral are set by the outside shape. You can tilt these spirals off-center by making the sides of the shape shorter on one side and longer on the other. The Baravelle spiral shown is off-center because the sides of the shape on the lower left side are shorter than the sides on the upper right.

Alternating Increments

Alternate longer and shorter increments on every other side. This variation keeps the spiral centered, but changes the shape as it moves toward the center. In a square spiral, the center changes to a diamond.

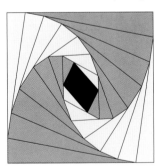 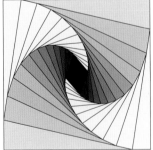

Alternating   Alternating + Perspective

Detail, Splish Splash Spirals
page 134

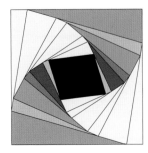 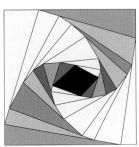 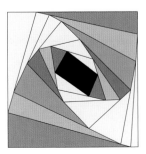

Random Increments

The more randomness you introduce into a spiral's increments or sides, the more irregular and whimsical it becomes. Surprisingly, however, the spiral technique still works as long as you mark the dots less than halfway along the side of the shape. The possibilities with this approach are unpredictable, so experiment to get a sense of the final result.

Pinwheel With Sawtooth Edges

*N*ormally when you draw a Pinwheel spiral (page 20), the lines cross the tips of the triangles, then you erase the bit of line that cuts the tip off. If instead you erase the tips of the triangles, you create a jagged edge that looks like a sawblade. You can make one, several, or all of the edges sawtooth. For the best effect, have sharply contrasting colors on both sides of the sawtooth edge. Sawtooth edges also require some small adjustments in the way the spiral is sewn (see *Sewing Sawtooth Edges and Avoiding Partial Seams (Pinwheel Spirals)*, page 99).

Sawtooth Edges With Bold Contrast

Strongly contrasting colors show off the sawtooth edges on all four spokes of these square Pinwheel spirals.

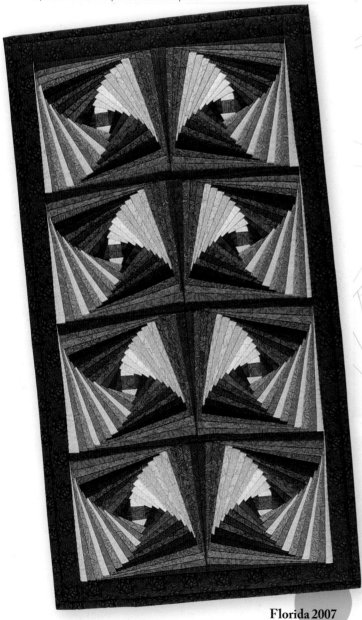

Florida 2007
16¾" × 30¼"
Designed, pieced and quilted by Susanne Schmid

Drawing Sawtooth Edges

Ring 1
1. *Lines crossed at corner*
2. *Erasing the line of the tip*
3. *Cut-off tip*

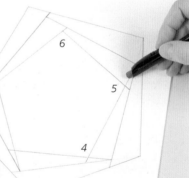

Ring 2
4. *Lines crossed at the corner*
5. *Erasing the line of the tip*
6. *Cut-off tips begin forming sawtooth edge*

Completed Spiral With Sawtooth Edges

Connecting Spirals

Trunks, Points and Fans

A spiral of any shape can connect smoothly to any other spiral if the connecting sides are the same length and the corners meet. When you place spirals side-by-side, the connecting spokes form three basic shapes: trunks, points and fans. Trunks, points and fans are particularly evident in spirals with three, four or five sides.

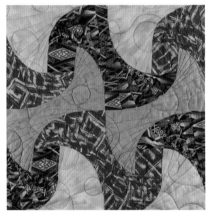  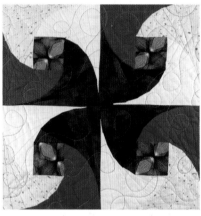

Trunks

Adjoining spirals form trunks when they spin in the same direction and adjacent spokes are the same color.

Points and Fans

Adjoining spirals form points and fans when they spin in the opposite directions. Fans and points are the same shape; fans have the curved side up and points have the curved side down.

Split Trunks, Points and Fans

When the color changes at the edge where blocks meet, the trunk, point or fan is split in half. Grouped together, these split forms can make flowers and stars.
All three details above are from:

Bev, Barb & a Bottle of Wine
page 142

Trunks, Points and Fans

The pairs of squares on the sides and top spin in the same direction, so they form trunks where they join. The half-square triangle spirals in the center are in mirrored pairs, so they form points and fans.

Mesclun Mixed
25½" × 25½"
Designed, pieced and quilted by Gail Wiebe

Ribbons

*R*ibbons are simply elongated points and fans. In shapes with more sides, the sides are shorter, so the spokes are narrower and more twisted.

Ribbons Formed With Eight-Sided Spirals
Connecting spokes of eight-sided Point-to-Point spirals.

Detail, Starry Night
page 69

Irregular Spirals With Points and Ribbons
Yellow fans, orange trunk points and purple and green ribbons form where these triangles and pentagons connect, even though the shapes are irregular.

Detail, Majestic Mandalai
page 140

Blue Ribbons
The spokes in this snowflake are trunks that flow like ribbons from the six-sided spiral in the center to five-sided spirals that surround it.

Detail, Do You See?
page 144

Baravelle Ribbons
Connecting spokes of eight-sided Baravelle spirals spinning in the same direction (right, top) and in opposite directions (right, bottom).

Detail, Synergy
page 126

Quilts With Combined Spirals in This Book

- Ellen's Star Rising *page 139*
- Florida 2007 *page 44*
- Hearts Form From Pieces *page 62*
- Hot & Cold *page 59*
- Northern Stars *page 36*
- Not My Dad's Bow Ties! *page 61*
- Oriental Fantasy *page 66*
- Plum Crazy *page 53*
- Ribbons of Life *page 62*
- Sails & Waves *page 136*
- Tropicale *page 63*
- We've Got Sisters! *page 102*
- Whirlygig *page 141*

Detail, Vestments for St. Bart's
page 67

Connecting Pinwheel and Point-to-Point Spirals

This section contains some technical information about combining spirals. If you'd rather stick to the basics, skip to *Centers and Surrounding Elements* (page 52), then return to this section later.

*P*inwheels and Point-to-Point spirals have *solid sides*: The outer triangles cover the entire side of the shape, so they naturally make a complete connection to each other.

Although these connections are usually the smoothest, they can be physically bulky, particularly when joining mirrored pairs. Many people prefer to use Nesting spirals instead, since they are less bulky at corners. That bulk is not necessarily a reason to avoid Pinwheel spirals. If they're right for your design, use them. When you join Pinwheel spirals, give them a shot of steam and whack the seams with a wooden mallet to smooth them.

Pinwheel Spirals Forming a Trunk **Pinwheel Spirals Forming a Point/Fan**

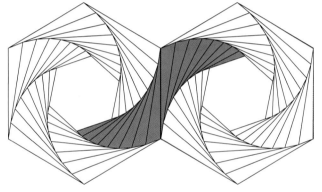 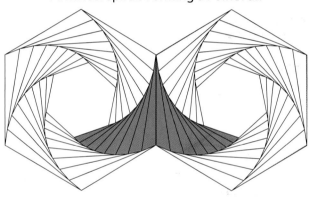

Pinwheel and Point-to Point
Pinwheels and Point-to-Point spirals have solid sides: The outer triangles cover the entire side of the shape, so they naturally make a complete connection to each other.

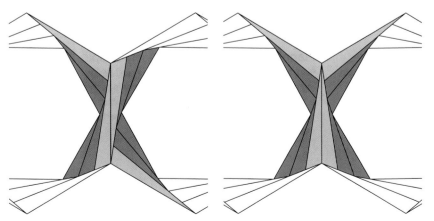

Another Solution for Bulky Points: Nesting Spirals With a Pinwheel Start
Draw only the first ring of triangles as a Pinwheel spiral (light gray) to make a strong connection between the spirals, then draw subsequent rings as Nesting spirals (dark gray).

Connecting Nesting and Baravelle Spirals

*N*esting and Baravelle spirals have *split sides*: The outer triangles only partially cover the side of the shape. Each side of the outside edge is partially covered by two triangles—one long side (gray in diagrams below), one short side (black in diagrams below). This can create some problems for connections, but there are solutions.

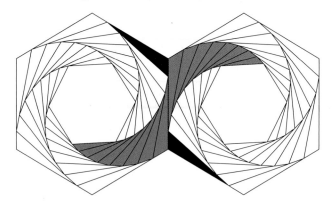

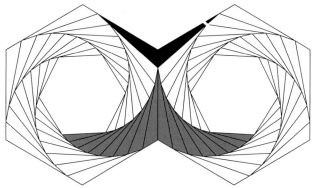

Nesting Spirals, Trunk Connection
Depending on the surrounding design, a trunk connection between Nesting spirals may be fine without modification. If a stronger connection is needed, use a pinwheel start (page 47) or sashing (page 49).

Nesting Spirals, Point/Fan Connection
In point/fan connections between Nesting spirals, the sides of the adjoining triangles must be the same length. In identical mirrored pairs, this happens naturally.

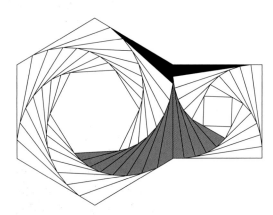

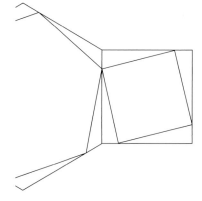

Dissimilar Spirals
If the adjoining spirals are not the same, the sides of adjoining triangles may not be the same length, interrupting the smooth flow from one spiral to the next.

Planning Connections for Dissimilar Spirals
Plan the connections when you draw your quilt design. Lay out adjoining shapes and draw the first ring of triangles in each shape. On the adjoining sides, where two spirals spin toward each other, use the same dot for both spirals. This will make the short sides of the triangles match, and flow smoothly.

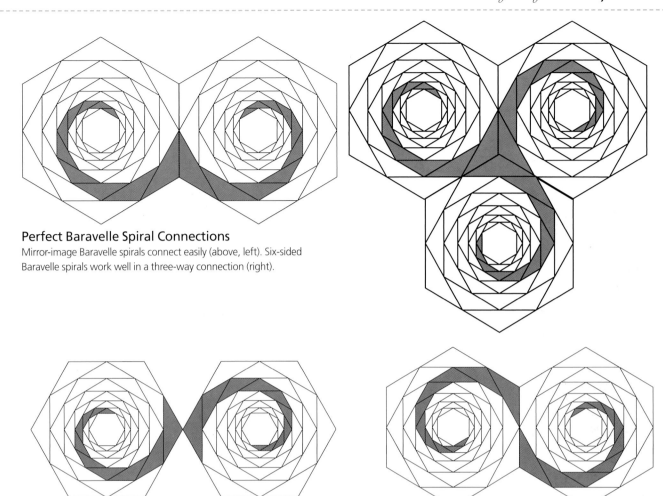

Perfect Baravelle Spiral Connections

Mirror-image Baravelle spirals connect easily (above, left). Six-sided Baravelle spirals work well in a three-way connection (right).

Problematic Baravelle Connections

When you try to connect same-direction Baravelle spirals, the triangles may not touch at all. This can happen whether the spirals meet at the points (above, left) or at the sides (above, right). But sashing can help these Baravelle spiral shapes connect.

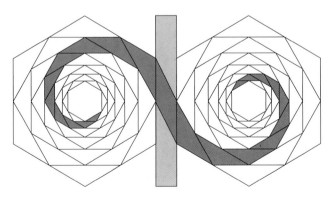

Sashing

The best way to connect same-direction Baravelle spirals is to add a sash with a diagonal connector. (This is the only way to smoothly connect eight-sided Baravelle spirals.) To draw this just lay the spirals over a piece of paper in the position you want, draw lines at the sides of the spirals, then draw connecting lines between the spokes. It will work at any angle.

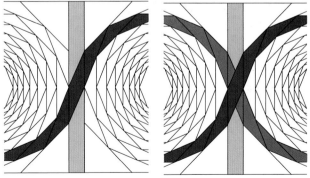

Diagonal Connections With Sashing

With the help of sashing, you can do a single diagonal connection (above, left) or a double diagonal one (above, right).

Double-Width Connections

ouble-width connections occur when you are working with gradations and two triangles of the same color connect in a mirrored pair creating a point or a fan. You can use this double-wide section as a design element, or adjust it using one of the methods shown here.

**Detail, Sails &
Waves**
page 136

Solution 1: Draw Edge Triangles Half as Wide

To avoid a double width connection when joining mirrored Pinwheel or Nesting spirals, make the increment distance on the outside triangles (the connecting edges) half the width of the increment for the other triangles in the spiral.

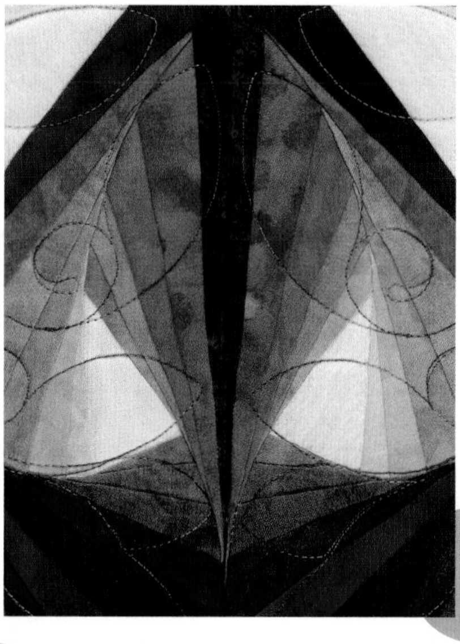

**Detail,
Northern Stars**
page 36

Double-Width Centers

If you're connecting a mirrored pair of spirals that creates a point or fan, and all the triangles are the same width, the two connecting triangles will create a center section in the point or fan that is twice as wide as the other triangles in the spiral. This will be most apparent in spirals with only a few sides.

Solution 2: Keep the Width, But Change the Color

You can eliminate a double-wide connection by changing colors at the edge of the adjoining spirals.

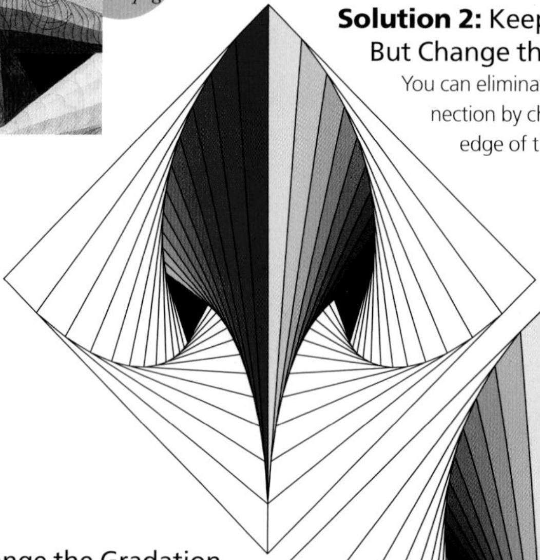

Solution 3: Change the Gradation

You can mask the double-width connection by coloring adjacent triangles with different shades of the same color in a gradation. This will make your design asymmetrical. In a Point-to-Point spiral the asymmetry will be obvious, because the triangles on the outside edges are quite large. In a Pinwheel or Nesting spiral the triangles are much narrower, so if the color difference is slight the asymmetry may not be apparent. In a repeated spiral pattern, make the same adjustment consistently and the asymmetry will become part of the pattern, a design element in itself that you may even decide to emphasize.

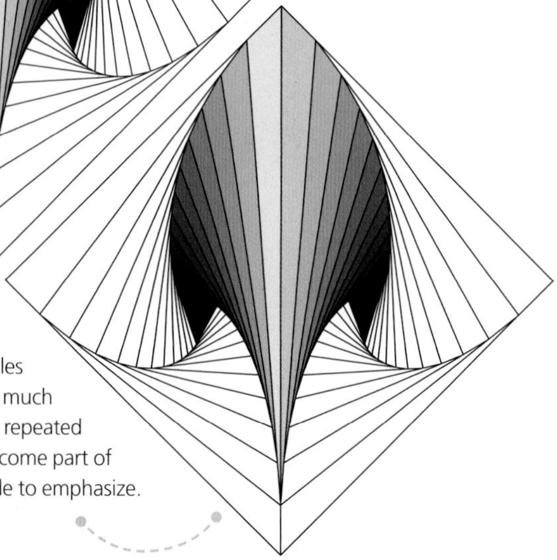

Bar Joins

*B*ar joins can occur when you connect two same-direction spirals to create a trunk. If you have the same color in adjoining triangles of connecting spokes, the two triangles will create a rectangular bar that may interrupt the flow of your design. This will be most apparent in spirals with few sides. If you like the effect, you can leave it alone or even highlight it. If you want to hide it, make the adjacent triangles different colors or different shades of the same color—the same solutions apply here as with double-width connections on the previous page. Even a slight difference in shade will break up the bar.

Solution 1: Let It Be

In trunk connections (page 45) with grada-tions, same-color adjoining triangles will form a bar. If you like the effect, you can leave it alone and make it part of a design, as in the quilt below.

Detail, Sails & Waves
page 136

Solution 2: Change the Gradation

You can hide a bar join by coloring the adjacent triangles with different shades or different colors.

Detail, Not My Dad's Bow Ties!
page 61

Spokes of a Wheel

In this quilt, the strong purple color in adjoin-ing triangles creates bar joins that become the central elements of design.

Brightly Churned
41" × 41"
Designed, sewn and quilted by Jill Kerekes

Centers and Surrounding Elements

*E*very spiral has a center. How will it relate to the spiral? Will it be small or large? Will it be a secondary element or will it be the focus with the spiral serving as a frame? The center can be solid, pieced, or even pictorial, as you'll see here.

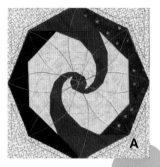

Detail, Fourth of July

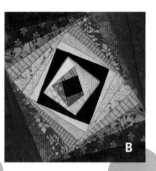

Detail, Ribbons
page 62

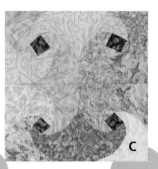

Detail, Gingkoesque
page 5

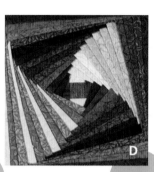

Detail, Florida 2007
page 44

Solid Centers

The simplest way to fill the center of a spiral is with a solid piece of fabric. It can match one or more of the spokes (A). If it matches the background, it looks like a cut-out (B). A contrasting color creates rhythm (C). Sometimes the role of the center is simply to go with the flow (D).

Other Quilts With Pieced Centers

● Infinite Rainbow *page 128*

● Exploding Spiral *page 112*

● Untitled (Red, White & Black) *page 58*

● Vestments for St. Bart's *page 67*

● Whirlygig *page 141*

Other Quilts With Pictorial Centers

● Crop Circles: How'd They Do That? *page 135*

● My Bloomin' Spiral *page 56*

● Photo Op?! *page 131*

● Vroom! Vroom! *page 55*

● Zowie! Powie! *page 120*

● Tropicale *page 63*

Pieced Centers

The only limits on pieced centers (right) are your imagination and how intricately you want to piece. Simple wedges are one possibility.

Detail, Holiday Whirl
page 24

Detail, Splish Splash Spirals
page 134

Spiral Frame
12" × 14"
Designed, sewn and quilted by Vicki Herrmann

Pictorial Centers

Placing a picture in the center of a spiral shifts the emphasis to the center and turns the spiral into a frame. After making *Vroom! Vroom!* (page 55) with a photo center, Vicki Herrmann thought it would be nice to be able to switch photos, so she designed this spiral calendar holder for interchangeable photos.

Plum Crazy
40" × 40"

Designed and sewn by Lois Hicks
Machine-quilted by Lorinda Graham

Centers and Corners

Lois used four eight-sided Baravelle spirals for her design, but what really makes it special are the centers and corners. Each of the adjoining corners of the spiral block are divided differently. When they join, they create different shapes that echo the pinwheels in the centers. The borders are simple, but also echo the checkerboard feel of the centers. Using only one color against black emphasizes the graphic strength of the design.

Fun Software

A fun way to create kaleidoscopic centers for your spirals is a software program called Kaleidoscope Kreator from Kaleidoscope Collections. You can use it to turn any photograph or scanned image into a circular kaleidoscope.

Corners

*I*f you are putting a round spiral in a square block, there will be empty space in the corners. This space offers the opportunity to create secondary patterns in your design.

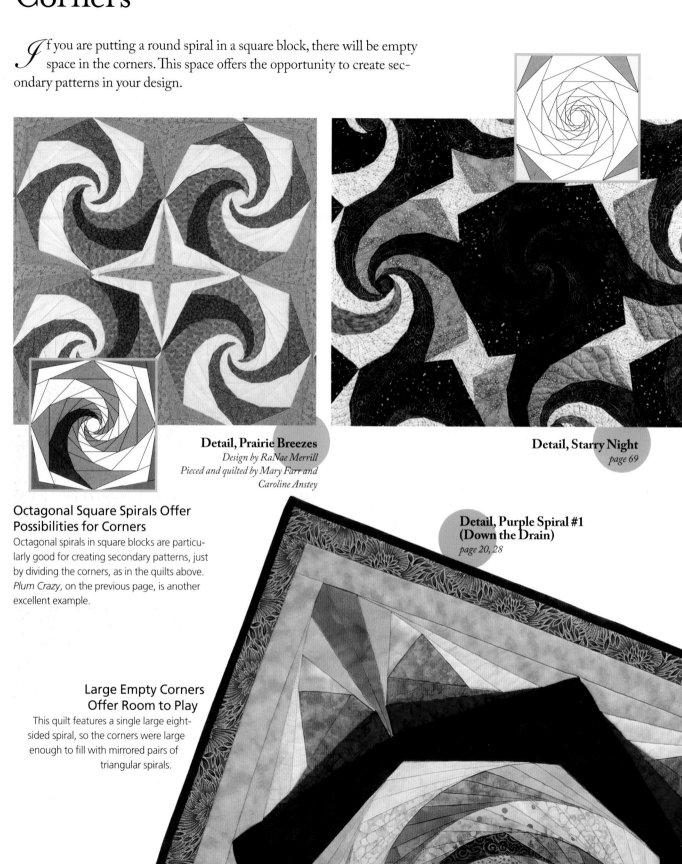

Detail, Prairie Breezes
Design by RaNae Merrill
Pieced and quilted by Mary Farr and
Caroline Anstey

Detail, Starry Night
page 69

**Detail, Purple Spiral #1
(Down the Drain)**
page 20, 28

Octagonal Square Spirals Offer Possibilities for Corners

Octagonal spirals in square blocks are particularly good for creating secondary patterns, just by dividing the corners, as in the quilts above. *Plum Crazy*, on the previous page, is another excellent example.

Large Empty Corners Offer Room to Play

This quilt features a single large eight-sided spiral, so the corners were large enough to fill with mirrored pairs of triangular spirals.

Surrounds and Backgrounds

To make a spiral fit into a square block or to finish a large spiral into a square quilt, spiral-piece the area around the spiral. Leave plenty of extra fabric beyond the finished size, then square up the block or quilt after sewing. This works either for spirals that touch the sides of the block or for spirals that float within it. A second option is to simply appliqué the spiral onto the background.

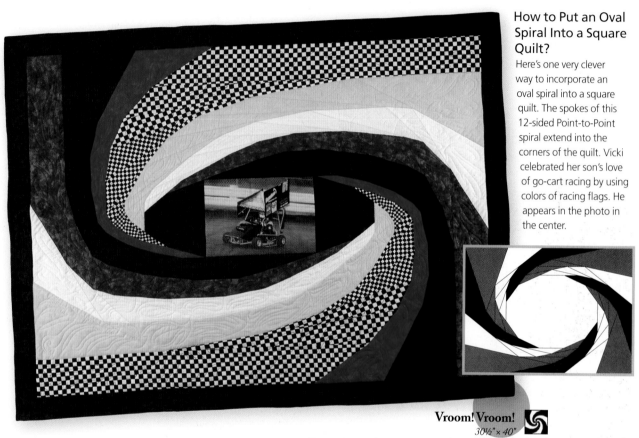

How to Put an Oval Spiral Into a Square Quilt?

Here's one very clever way to incorporate an oval spiral into a square quilt. The spokes of this 12-sided Point-to-Point spiral extend into the corners of the quilt. Vicki celebrated her son's love of go-cart racing by using colors of racing flags. He appears in the photo in the center.

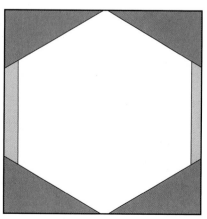

Vroom! Vroom!
30½" × 40"

Designed, sewn and machine-quilted by Vicki Herrman
Photo: Ryan Northcote

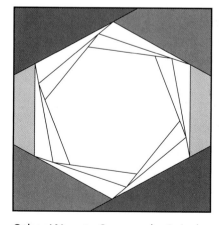
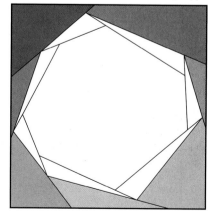

Other Ways to Surround a Spiral
Here are three more methods for piecing the area around the central spiral.

Single Setting

*S*ingle setting spiral quilts are made with a single large spiral. This is the simplest layout, because there is only one spiral to draw and sew.

Other Quilts With Single-Setting Layouts

- City Tears to Country Smiles *page 130*
- Exploding Spiral *page 112*
- Holiday Whirl *page 24*
- Infinite Rainbow *page 128*
- Photo Op?! *page 129*
- Spiral of Life *page 131*
- Vroom! Vroom! *page 55*
- Winged Water *page 33*

Gorgeous Centerpiece
A fourteen-sided Baravelle spiral in an oval surrounds broderie perse flowers.

My Bloomin' Spiral
40" × 45"
Designed, pieced, appliquéd and machine-quilted by Linda Cooper

Free Setting

*F*ree-set spiral quilts use multiple spirals, but the spirals do not connect with each other in the design. The quilts here show single spirals made in blocks, which are then placed in a free-set design.

Spiral and Non

Square Nesting spirals (above)—traditionally known as Twisted Log Cabin blocks—are combined here with Drunkard's Path blocks. The border is made of pieced Drunkard's Path blocks.

One Block, Five Roses

Square blocks containing irregular five-sided nesting spirals (left) are colored in rings to create dancing roses. The same block is flipped and rotated for variety.

Flying Tumbleweeds 🌀
69½" × 87"
Designed and sewn by Joan Garland
Machine-quilted by Peggy Barkle

🌀 **Roses Are My Best Friends**
12½" × 41"
Designed, sewn and machine-quilted by
Sandra Mettler

Other Quilts With Free Settings

● Big Bang + One Second *page 16*

● Good, Gracious Great Ball of Fire! *page 138*

● The Court Jester *page 116*

● Splish Splash Spirals *page 134*

Free Setting Using Appliqué

*Y*ou can place spirals in a free setting by appliquéing them into a design.

Extend Beyond the Background

Appliqué is an effective way to let the six-sided Nesting spirals extend beyond the rectangular background.

Spiro Pony From Texas
47" × 43½"
Designed and pieced by Roxanne Bowling
Machine-quilted by Helen King

Appliqué Details

The creators of this quilt are from Texas, where painted ponies are a big deal. They also like landscape quilts, so they "painted" the pony and the sun with appliquéd spirals.

Untitled (Red, White & Black)
14½" × 31½"
Designed, pieced and quilted by Gail Wiebe

Other Quilts With Appliqué

- Crop Circles: How'd They Do That? *page 135*

- In Memory of Marja *page 133*

- Spiral Pansies *page 35*

- Whirlpool Galaxy: A Glorious Creation *page 71*

Overlap Spirals

This quilter made each 3-inch petal with a triangle Nesting spiral, which she faced for a curved edge. She overlapped the petals to form the three-dimensional flower and added a rhinestone pin for the center.

Sustenance
13" × 15"
Designed, sewn and machine-quilted by Crystal Marie

Flow Setting, Single-Shape

*F*low-set spiral quilts use multiple spirals that connect to each other to create trunks, fans, points, ribbons and kaleidoscopic effects.

One way to approach a flow setting is to use all spirals of the same shape. Squares, rectangles, diamonds, right-angle triangles, equilateral triangles and hexagons are all shapes that, used by themselves, can completely fill the surface of your quilt with no spaces in between. Octagons, with the corners filled out to squares, are also ideal for single-shape flow settings. Experiment with the direction that the spirals spin—the same direction, opposite directions, mirrored pairs—to find a placement of trunks, points and fans you love.

Single-Shape Flow
A simple on-point block setting is made dramatic with spirals and sharply contrasting colors.

Hot & Cold
29" × 29"
Designed by Angelika Isler Meyer
Pieced and quilted by Susanne Schmid

Other Quilts With Single-Shape Flow Settings

- Bev, Barb and a Bottle of Wine *page 142*
- Florida 2007 *page 44*
- Grandpa Shirts *page 40*
- Northern Stars *page 36*
- Oriental Fantasy *page 66*
- Plum Crazy *page 53*
- Sails & Waves *page 136*
- Starry Night *page 69*
- Synergy *page 124*

Flow Setting, Multiple-Shape

Flow settings can use a single shape as on the previous page, but they can also use a variety of shapes, combining types of spirals and even non-spiral elements.

To create a multi-shape flow setting, begin with the shape you want your finished quilt to be. Divide it into any shapes you want. Place a spiral in each shape. Remember, flow settings work best when the connecting sides of the spirals are the same length and the corners meet. Experiment with the direction the spirals spin—the same direction, opposite directions, mirrored pair—until the placement is just right.

Multiple-Shape Flow
Spirals in two different triangles and a pentagon combine in a multiple-shape flow setting to make this unusual quilt.

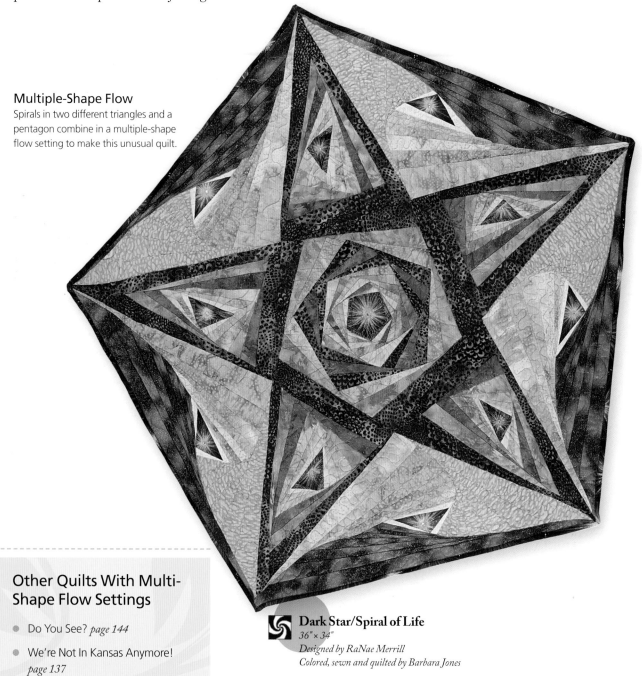

Other Quilts With Multi-Shape Flow Settings

- Do You See? *page 144*
- We're Not In Kansas Anymore! *page 137*

Dark Star/Spiral of Life
36" × 34"
Designed by RaNae Merrill
Colored, sewn and quilted by Barbara Jones

Block-as-Quilt Setting

*B*lock-as-quilt settings are a type of multiple-shape flow setting that uses a single block as the underlying structure for the quilt. They can include both flow-set and free-set spirals. The best blocks for block-as-quilt settings have patches with sides the same length and corners that meet.

(Electric Quilt-users, try doing this with Electric Quilt 6's Block-turned-Quilt layouts.)

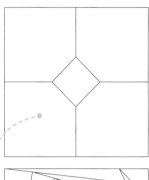

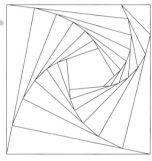

Not My Dad's Bow Ties!
26" × 26"
Designed, sewn and quilted by Kathy Edwards

Bow Tie Block

The underlying design in this quilt is a Bow Tie block. The blue sides of the bow tie are Pinwheel spirals and the black sides are Point-to-Point spirals. When four Bow Tie blocks were placed together, the large triangles in the center formed a Pinwheel, so Kathy filled it with a large print cut stack-and-whack style. In the Pinwheel spirals she gradated the blue from light to dark in some spokes and dark to light in others. The result looks like a three-dimensional bow in the Bow Tie block—a very happy coincidence.

Other Quilts With Block-as-Quilt Settings

See the next page, and also these quilts:

- Ellen's Star Rising *page 139*
- Good Gracious Great Ball of Fire! *page 138*
- Majestic Mandalai *page 140*

More Block-as-Quilt Settings

Diamond-in-the-Square Block

The layout of this quilt is based on the traditional Diamond-in-the-Square design. Patches are filled with a variety of square and half-square Nesting spirals. Even though the spirals flow into each other, Sandy changed colors at the edges of many of the spiral blocks, creating a line that keeps the original structure visible.

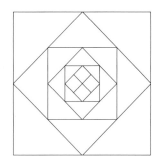

Ribbons of Life
70" × 70"
Designed and pieced by Sandy Weber
Quilted by John Liddicoat

Squares and Diamonds

The underlying structure of this quilt is a traditional-looking block made of squares and diamonds. Laurie placed a Pinwheel spiral in each patch of the block, but placed the same colors at adjoining edges, which obscures the square structure. Hearts and ribbons seem to dance across the surface, and Laurie's hand-dyed gradations add a three-dimensional effect.

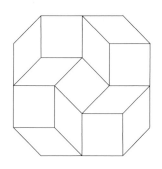

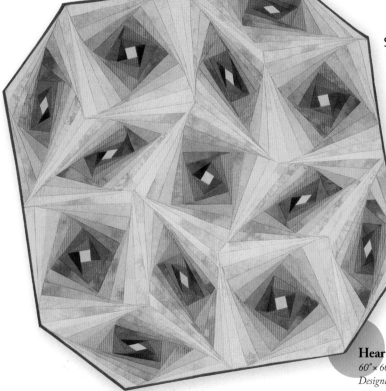

Hearts Form From Pieces
60" × 60"
Designed, sewn and quilted by Laurie Nathan

Mandalas

Mandala is the Sanskrit word for an intricate, usually circular design used in Buddhist religions. Creating a mandala is a form of worship or meditation (something that many quilters can relate to). The idea for mandala spiral quilts came to me one day while looking at the round stained-glass window in a church.

Where spiral quilts are concerned, mandalas are another type of multi-shape flow setting, though it's possible to place free-set spirals in them as well (see *Ellen's Star Rising*, page 139).

Begin drawing a mandala with a circle. Cut the circle into wedges, like a pie. There can be any number of wedges, but if you want a symmetrical design, use an even number. Cut across the wedges either straight or diagonally to create triangles and other shapes. Then place spirals in each shape and experiment!

Other Quilts With Mandalas

- Brightly Churned *page 51*
- Ellen's Star Rising *page 139* (also a block-as-quilt)
- Majestic Mandalai *page 140*

Tropical Memories

Each wedge of this mandala is made up of two different triangles and an irregular five-sided shape. The wedges are in mirrored pairs. Mary chose colors and fabrics that reminded her of New Zealand.

Tropicale
43½" × 43½"
Designed, pieced and quilted by Mary Reddington

Spirals Within Spirals

A spiral within a spiral is another type of multi-shape flow setting. Think of it as setting part of a design with smaller spirals, then circling them with a larger spiral.

The two quilts on these pages replace some of the rings of a twelve-sided spiral with a circle of smaller spirals. *Whirlygig* (page 141) uses eight triangle spirals as a pieced center, then circles them with an eight-sided spiral with feathered spokes.

Point-to-Point around Nesting Spirals

This quilt designer was inspired by Stonehenge and other stone circles found throughout the United Kingdom. The sun design begins in the center with a twelve-sided Point-to-Point spiral colored as a sunburst (see *Sunbursts*, page 36). It is surrounded by a ring of twelve triangle Nesting spirals representing the months of the year. The outer rings are a continuation of the inner Point-to-Point spiral, now with feathered spokes. The stones are appliquéd in silhouette over the spiral.

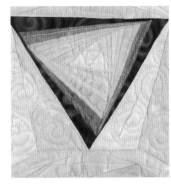

Detail

Midsummer
42" × 56"
Designed and sewn by Devi Lanphere
Machine-quilted by Gwen Baggett

Point-to-Point around Baravelle Spirals

The moon design begins in the center with a twelve-sided Point-to-Point spiral colored in rings. It is surrounded with a ring of twelve square Baravelle spirals, which is then surrounded by a continuation of the inner spiral, again colored in rings. The shadows of the stones are quilted in six shades of gray thread.

Detail

Midwinter
40" × 54"
Designed and sewn by Devi Lanphere
Machine-quilted by Gwen Baggett

Spiral Borders

*Y*ou can use spirals by themselves or combined with other elements to create stunning borders for any quilt.

Since spirals will fit in any shape, they can easily accommodate every border length. Measure the length of the sides of the quilt and divide it into an equal number of sections. Use square blocks in the corners. Leave the sections rectangular or subdivide them into other shapes. Draw spirals of any configuration you wish in the sections. Experiment with the direction that the spirals spin—the same direction, opposite directions, mirrored pairs—to find a placement of trunks, points and fans that you love.

Other Quilts With Spiral Borders

- Ribbons of Life *page 62*
- Sails & Waves *page 138*

Fan Border

Square Pinwheel spirals in mirrored pairs form the fans in this border. Katie chose printed fabrics that gradually blend red into black. Contrasting gold in the outer triangles on two sides create the wave effect.

Oriental Fantasy
38″ × 38″
Designed, sewn and quilted by Katie Fields Appliqué design by Geri Richardson of Grannie 'G' Appliqué

Twisting Ribbons Border

I made these vestments for the associate rector at St. Bart's Episcopal Church in New York City. The spirals are eight-sided Baravelle spirals. The mirrored pair in the hem are 5½-inch square. Similar spirals on the sleeves and the stole are 3¼-inch square. Each contains seventy-seven pieces. The spirals combine with a design of twisting ribbons inspired by the stonework in the church.

Vestments for St. Bart's
Designed and sewn by RaNae Merrill

Two Possibilities for Spiral Borders

In the examples below, top is made of right-angle triangles spinning the same direction set into squares; then the squares are set in mirrored pairs. To turn the corner, the corner square has mirrored right-angle triangles. In the bottom example, Baravelle spirals are colored with interwoven double spokes. Sashing makes a smooth connection between spirals.

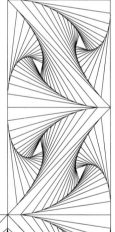

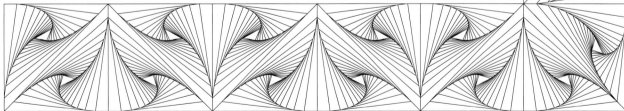

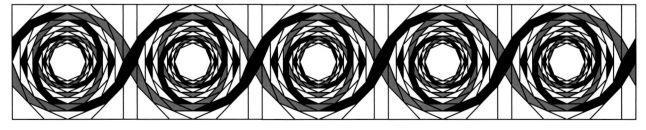

Choosing Colors and Fabrics

*C*hoosing fabrics for a spiral is a balancing act between *blend* and *separation*. To make each spoke hold together as a unit, you need fabrics that blend. To define different spokes, you need fabrics that separate. The differences come down to three factors: *color*, *value* and *pattern*.

Color

Begin by choosing the overall color scheme for your quilt. Inspiration can come from many sources: your home décor, a wonderful fabric, a theme (like red and green for Christmas) or perhaps a place you have visited. I often choose three or four colors that mix nicely and then add a "kicker"—one color that doesn't quite mix with all the rest. A small amount of the kicker adds punctuation and excitement. In *The Court Jester* (page 116), orange is the kicker.

Same Spiral, Different Colors and Fabrics
Your fabric and color choices will have an enormous effect on the look of your quilt. The same spiral can appear completely different depending on the colors and fabrics you choose. Each of these spirals has the same structure, but the fabrics change their characters completely.

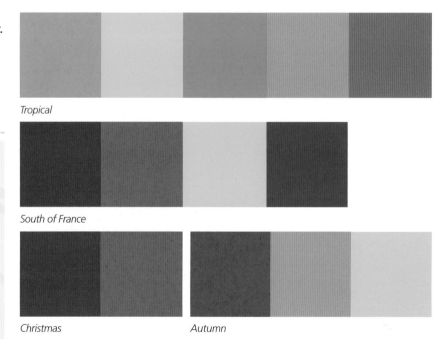

Tropical

South of France

Christmas   *Autumn*

Color Schemes and Color Theory
Learning about color theory—the science of how colors work together—can be a big help in choosing a pleasing color scheme. There are many excellent books and websites on color theory; several are listed in Recommended Reading at the end of this book.

Key Questions When Choosing Colors and Fabrics

When you think about color and fabric, some questions to ask yourself are:

- Do I want sharply-defined spokes or a softer, sparkly-looking spiral?

- Do I want my spirals to appear three-dimensional?

- Do I want to want to emphasize the shape or the spokes?

Values

After you choose your overall color scheme, the next step is choosing individual fabrics within that scheme. This starts with consideration of *value*. Value describes how light or dark the colors are. You will need a variety of lights, mediums and darks for your spiral quilt.

Similar values have low contrast; they blend areas. Differing values have medium or high contrast; they separate areas. Where you place the lights and darks is essential to how (or even whether) the structure of the design will appear. Place fabrics with low contrast in areas you want to blend. Place high-contrast fabrics in areas you want to separate and define.

Values in Black and White
Pure colors have different values, even before you begin making them lighter or darker. Here's the rainbow in both color and black and white, to show value.

Medium Values
It's easiest to see value when you eliminate color. Notice how medium values can appear either light or dark, depending on whether they are placed next to dark or light.

Contrasting Values
This quilt uses a fairly monochromatic palette, so the overall design is mainly defined by value and varying degrees of contrast

Some Tricks for Seeing Value

Here are a few ways you can compare fabrics in black and white to see only value and contrast:

- Squint your eyes
- View the fabrics through a piece of transparent red plastic; this reduces colors to value only
- Photocopy, photograph or scan the fabrics in black and white (label them so you can tell them apart without color)

Starry Night
46" × 46"
Designed and pieced by Jamie McClenaghan
Machine-quilted by Gwen Baggett

More Choosing Colors and Fabrics

Go slowly through the fabric examples on the next few pages. Study each one until you absorb the concept it teaches. Take this information with you on your next trip to the fabric store.

*T*he last factor to consider in choosing fabrics is *pattern*. Patterns add texture and scale to your spiral quilt. They can communicate an idea or a theme, or even add a bit of humor. As you make your own fabric choices, look through the quilts in this book to observe how other quilters have used pattern in their designs.

Solids and Pseudo-Solids

Solid colors, monochrome textures or tone-on-tone prints create solid spokes with clearly defined edges. Since there is little or no pattern to deal with, these work well in either large or small triangles of a spoke.

Multicolor Fabrics

The best multicolor fabrics for spirals have small- to medium-size patterns that are fairly dense, have evenly distributed colors and are non-directional. Large or widely spread patterns may work, but might require fussy-cutting and careful placement. Remember that in most cases you'll be cutting fabrics in narrow triangles, and you want the pattern to be seen as much as possible within that small space.

Think of multicolor fabrics as having a dominant color and one or more secondary colors. The dominant color is the main color of the fabric. If there is a background color, that is the dominant color.

In a multicolor fabric, dominant colors set the overall color scheme of the quilt design. If their colors and values are similar, they will blend. To the degree that their colors and values contrast, they will separate.

Secondary colors in a multicolor fabric can strengthen or weaken blends and separations. You can also use same or similar secondary colors to relate contrasting fabrics, which helps hold together your overall design. If their purpose is to separate, limit secondary colors in a fabric to one or two. Since there are only six colors (besides neutrals black, brown and white), using too many in one fabric leaves few color options for the other fabrics.

Also keep your eye on the ratio of dominant to secondary colors in patterns. Even though several fabrics may have the same dominant and secondary colors, if the proportions of the colors vary, their overall values will be different. (This is exactly what you want for gradations. See *Gradation of Color and Value*, page 76.)

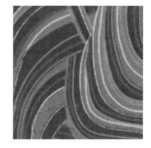

Dominant color: Green
Secondary colors: Purple, Yellow

Dominant color: Ivory
Secondary colors: Red, Green

Dominant and Secondary Colors

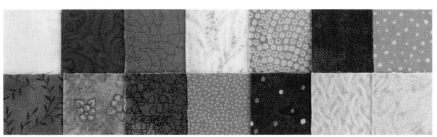

Solids and Pseudo-Solids
Notice how adjacent swatches blend where there are similar values and separate where there are different values.

Placing Colors and Values in a Spiral

*H*ow strong or subtle do you want the spiral effect to be in your design? Use fabrics that separate—different values, colors and patterns—for a clearly defined spiral. Use fabrics that blend—similar values, colors and patterns—to hold spokes together, and for a softer spiral effect.

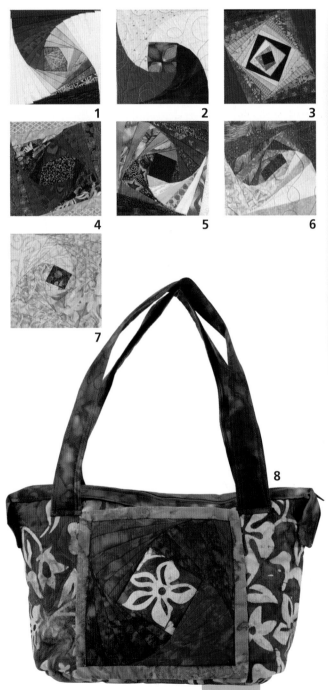

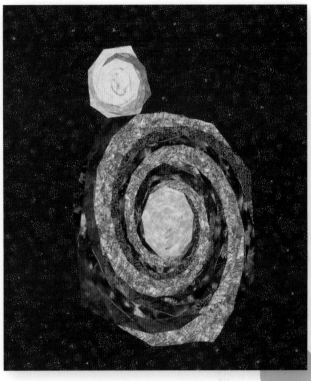

Whirlpool Galaxy, A Glorious Creation
32½" × 38"
Designed, sewn and quilted by Becky Bozic

Mixing Color, Value and Placement

This quilt has an effective mix of color, value and pattern. In order to suggest a starry galaxy, Becky choose a variety of busy prints, some that separate, some that blend. She used the same or blending fabrics within each spoke to hold it together. To vary the width of the spokes, she used the same or blending fabrics in some adjacent spokes. To separate spokes, she used fabrics with strong differences of value. Compare the use of color and pattern in this quilt above to *Starry Night* (page 69).

Value Placement

Placement of value and pattern within a spiral changes its shape, and emphasizes or hides the spiral effect.

1. *Alternating light and dark between spokes.*

2. *Adjacent lights, adjacent darks.*

3. *Darks around the edge, lights near center.*

4. *Light at sides and color-to-color gradations.*

5. *Blending patterns within spokes.*

6, 7, 8. *Busy patterns and similar values obscure separation between spokes and hide the overall spiral designs.*

It's My Bag
Designed, pieced and quilted by Beth Bigler
Pattern by Joan Hawley, Lazy Girl Designs

Fabrics that Blend

When you want to hold together areas of a design—such as within a single spoke—use fabrics that blend. Notice in the examples on this page that even though the colors are sometimes different, each pair of swatches is blended by the same value. Value, even more than color, enables fabrics to blend.

The examples on these two pages are arranged in eight groups. The pairings in Group 1 offer maximum blending; those in Group 8 offer maximum separation. Each pair of fabrics demonstrates different ways in which colors can interact and affect value. Look at them one pair at a time to really understand what is happening. (Cover up the rest with a sheet of paper.)

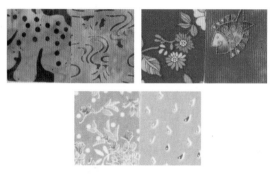

1 Same Dominant, Same Secondary, Same Value (SSS)
Maximum Blending • Good in Spokes

Identical dominant colors, secondary colors and value give each pair of these fabrics the strongest blend. Each pair is also similar in scale. They seem like they could be different sections of the same fabric.

2 Same Dominant, Different Secondary, Same Value (SDS)
High Blending • Good in Spokes

Each of these pairs of fabric share the same dominant color and same value, so the different secondary colors seem to flow into one another. Mixing fabrics like these in a single spoke would be an interesting way to add color and texture while still holding it firmly together. They are perfect for gradations (see page 76) because they change color without a hard line between fabrics.

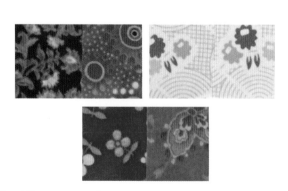

3 Different Dominant, Same Secondary, Same Value (DSS)
Medium Blending • Good in Gradations

In these pairs you can see the separation between different dominant colors, yet it is softened by the same secondary colors and value. (Red and green have the same value, which is why the patterns of Christmas quilts are sometimes difficult to see.) In the top right example, both fabrics are the exact same design, only the lines change from blue to orange.

4 Different Dominant, Different Secondary, Same Value (DDS)
Medium Blending • Good in Gradations

Though these pairs have different dominant and secondary colors, having the same value still makes them seem more similar than different. Notice in the top right pair how the large spot of color in the right swatch makes the fabric on the left seem to overlap it, softening the dividing line between the two fabrics.

Fabrics that Separate

When you want to contrast areas of a design—such as adjacent spokes—use fabrics that separate. Notice in the examples on this page that even though the colors are sometimes the same, each pair of swatches is separated by differing values. Value, even more than color, makes fabrics separate.

5 Same Dominant, Same Secondary, Different Value (SSD)

Medium to Low Separation • Good in Gradations

This group shows how changes in value can happen in different ways. In the top left pair, the dominant color is the same, but it has different values in the two fabrics. Since the secondary colors are the same color and value, there is little contrast. In the top right pair, dominant and secondary colors are the same, but the introduction of white into the second pattern gives it a lighter value. In the bottom pair, dominant and secondary colors are the same, but the proportions of the colors are different, which changes the value.

6 Same Dominant, Different Secondary, Different Value (SDD)

Medium to Low Separation • Good in Gradations

Here are more examples of how changes in value can happen in different ways. In the top left pair, the dominant color is the same, but it has different values in the two fabrics. In the top right pair, the dominant color is identical, but the red is a strong secondary color that changes the value. In the bottom pair, the dominant colors are the same but have different values, and the secondary colors are different.

7 Different Dominant, Same Secondary, Different Value (DSD)

Strong to Medium Separation • Good in Adjacent Spokes

Though dominant colors and values separate these fabrics, the entire group is held together by pink as a secondary color. Similar personalities also strengthen the unity. This would be an ideal group for the *Exploding Spiral* project on page 112.

8 Different Dominant, Different Secondary, Different Value (DDD)

Strongest Separation • Good in Adjacent Spokes

Everything is different about these pairs, and yet they still go together. Why? First, the patterns or textures are similar. Second, the top left and bottom pairs are complementary colors. Third, the top right pair in the middle is what I call an inversion: The dominant color of one is a secondary color of the other.

A Few More Fabric Considerations

Fabric "Personalities"

Beyond color and value, patterns have personalities. Like people, fabrics often need similar styles in order to get along. Personality factors can include such things as scale (large versus small), structure (random versus geometric), era (vintage versus modern), theme (florals versus trucks), style (batik versus stripe) and busy-ness (lots of color and pattern versus solid or tone-on-tone). If you use only a few fabrics or very large pieces, select fabrics with similar personalities. The more fabrics you mix up, the more personalities dilute each other, so personality becomes less important.

Pattern Size or Scale

Patterns on fabric can be small, medium or large. As you select fabrics, keep in mind the size of the pattern relative to the size of your spiral. A small spiral needs solids or small patterns. A large spiral can accommodate larger patterns. As you consider fabrics, look at them in small, medium and large pieces to see how the pattern will fit in the small, medium and large triangles of your spiral. Sometimes even if the overall design is large, there are areas with enough detail that you can fussy-cut smaller pieces to get the color and pattern you want in smaller areas of your spiral.

Some Personalities Clash
Because purple isn't associated with Christmas, the purple clashes with the Christmas novelty print (A). The loose, random design and lime green background clash with the structured, regal pattern in gold (B). The darker colors on the left (C) seem far too serious for the bubbly purple pattern.

Quilts With Large-Scale Fabrics

- Majestic Mandalai *page 140*
- Mesclun Mixed *page 45*
- My Bloomin' Spiral *page 56*
- Not My Dad's Bow Ties! *page 61*
- Tannenbaum Twist *page 115*

Contained and Loose Effects
If a pattern is too large or too loose, it may be difficult to create a cohesive spoke, because there is not enough of the same color in each triangle. Place a contrasting color or small-scale fabric next to a fabric with a larger print if you want to contain it (above, left). On the other hand, a loose, floating effect might be just what you want (above, right).

Gradation of Size

*J*ust as you can do gradations of value and color in a spiral (see *Gradation of Color and Value,* page 76), you can also do gradations of pattern size. The most natural direction is from small in the center to large at the outer edge, but you can do it any way you like. Gradation of pattern helps create a sense of perspective, which can be even more pronounced if you go from small/dark to large/light.

Checkerboards
Occasionally, you'll find an identical pattern in different sizes. Look at *Vroom! Vroom!* (page 55) to see how these graduated checkerboard fabrics communicate a sense of speed and distance.

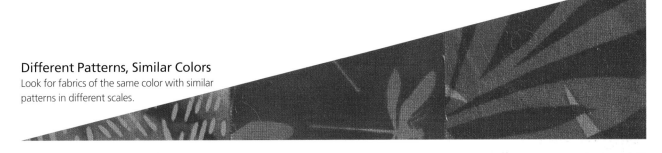

Different Patterns, Similar Colors
Look for fabrics of the same color with similar patterns in different scales.

Pattern Collections
Sometimes manufacturers make coordinating patterns of different sizes in the same collection, like the two purple fabrics (middle and right), both from a collection by Quilting Treasures/Cranston. Notice also how the colors go from darker in the smallest print to lighter in the largest one.

One-Stop Shopping
Every now and then you find a wonderful fabric like this one from Hoffman that does all the size and color gradation for you. The actual width of this sample is 44".

Gradation of Color and Value

*S*pirals lend themselves beautifully to using gradated values and colors, simply make each triangle in a spoke gradually different in value, color or both.

You can use gradation to create the illusion of three dimensions. Dark areas recede and light areas advance, so place dark fabrics where you want depth or distance and light fabrics where you want height or proximity.

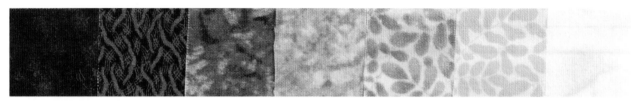

Value Gradation
Try a gradation of different values of the same color, from dark to light.

Inversion Gradation
Do a gradation of patterned fabrics from one dominant/ secondary color pairing to its opposite. This inversion gradation starts start with red dominant and yellow secondary, and gradually transitions to a fabric with yellow dominant and red secondary. For color gradations, there will usually be one fabric in the middle that has equal proportions of all the colors in the mix—this is the "pivot" fabric.

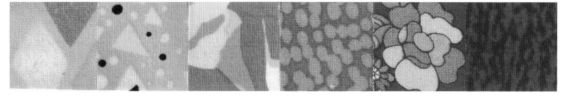

Color-to-Color Gradation
Use patterns to shift from one color to a completely different color. Increase the amount of the secondary color, then shift the dominant, or background, color.

Other Quilts Using Color Gradation

- Big Bang + One Second *page 16*
- Northern Stars *page 36*
- Not My Dad's Bow Ties *page 61*
- Sails & Waves *page 136*
- Ribbons of Life *page 62*
- Infinite Rainbow *page 128*
- We've Got Sisters *page 100*
- Sustenance *page 58*
- We're Not In Kansas Anymore *page 137*
- Tropicale *page 63*

Placing Gradations in a Spiral

You can gradate value, color and/or size in all the ways shown here.
Try these and do your own experimentation.

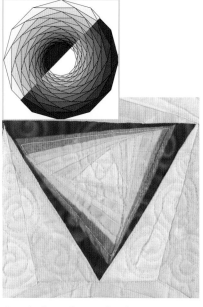

Gradation Within Spokes
Gradate within one or more individual spokes of a spiral.

Gradation Across Spokes
Gradate across spokes in a single spiral.

Gradation Through Rings
Gradate through rings in a single spiral, either center to edge or edge to center. If you gradate all spokes of a spiral in the same direction, but use different colors in different spokes, the effect will be similar to gradating through rings (see *Ribbons of Life*, page 62).

Flow Gradation
Gradate in single spokes flowing across adjoining spirals.

Split Flow Gradation
Flow gradation, splitting at the adjoining edge.

Directional and Radial Fabrics

*E*very piece of fabric in a spiral has a different orientation, so using stripes, geometrics and directional prints in spirals presents a design question: Do they interrupt or heighten the spinning effect? Place them carefully to get the effect you want.

Radial Designs

Radial designs are becoming more common in the market, and work wonderfully in spirals. Fussy-cut them so that the radiating lines fit into the tips of the triangles in a spoke, or find your own creative way to position them in your design. *Majestic Mandalai* (page 140) makes effective use of the same radial design in its center, spirals and borders.

Border Prints

Border prints are usually large and have direction. Treat them as a hybrid of a large pattern and a stripe. Fussy-cut and place carefully. They can unify a design if used in both spirals and borders.

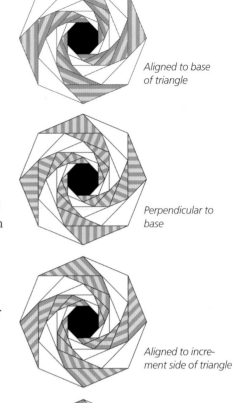

Aligned to base of triangle

Perpendicular to base

Aligned to increment side of triangle

Aligned to outer edge of triangle

Directional Fabrics
These fabrics stand out against softer patterns. Use their direction for specific design effects.

Enhance the Spiral
If you want to use directional fabrics to heighten the spiral effect, consider these ways (above) of positioning them in the spiral.

Radials
Fabrics such as large-scale florals, Japanese fan prints, tie dyes and Australian Aboriginals offer interesting possibilities when carefully cut and placed in a spiral. My own Radiant Collection fabrics for Blank Quilting (far left) were created specifically with spirals in mind, The diagram at right shows how each of the fabrics might fit into the spokes of the spiral.

Color Charts

As you develop your design (particularly if you are using many different fabrics) you may find it helpful to create a color chart. A color chart can take many forms—a mock-up of the spiral itself, rows of fabric swatches like the one shown here or a pie shape are all possibilities.

A color chart will help you determine a variety of things before you sew (possibly saving you time, money and ultimately from disappointment):

- Do the colors complement each other?
- Do fabrics have enough blend or separation to show the design?
- Do the patterns and personalities of the fabrics work together?
- Are the sizes of the patterns right for the design?
- Are gradations smooth and even?

Color Chart for *We're Not In Kansas Anymore* (page 137)
Each row represents one of the ten spokes in the central spiral. Spokes alternate solid and gradated.

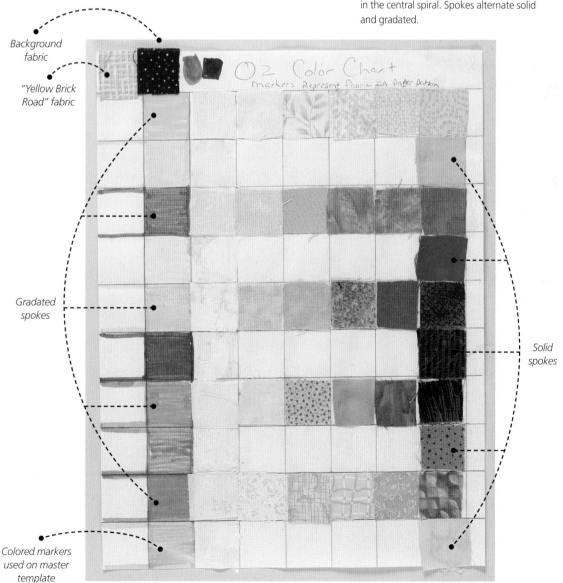

Background fabric

"Yellow Brick Road" fabric

Gradated spokes

Colored markers used on master template

Solid spokes

Starry Night
page 69

Chapter 3

Sewing Spirals

In the previous chapter, you explored ways to design and plan a spiral quilt. Once you have a design plan, you are ready to turn it into a quilt. This chapter will take you step-by-step from plan to finished quilt.

Since spirals are foundation-pieced, the first step is to prepare your foundations. Next, figure your yardage needs, gather your fabrics and cut.

And then, you sew: First assemble the individual spirals, then join spirals and other sections of the quilt. Quilt and bind and—*voilà!*—your spiral quilt is done. I hope you'll enjoy the process and be proud of the result!

Preparing Foundations

How Foundation Piecing Works

Spirals are sewn with foundation piecing. This means that the pattern is drawn on paper or a lightweight material like interfacing—the foundation—then the fabric is sewn to the foundation, using the drawn lines as the seam lines. Because the lines on the paper guide the seams, it is not necessary to cut fabric accurately and match seam allowances. Once the spiral is sewn, a paper foundation is torn away, while a fabric foundation can be left in. If you'd like to learn more about foundation piecing techniques, see the books under *Resources* on page 145.

Tools and Materials for Making Foundations

- *Straightedge/ruler:* one with an edge that lays on the surface of the paper, not a raised edge. Accurate, easy-to-read markings are important. Get one long enough for the spiral you're drawing and easy to manage, because you'll be moving it around a lot.
- *Mechanical pencils:* better than wood pencils because they remain sharp. I like ones with a narrow metal shaft to carry the lead at the tip because they write closest to the straightedge.

- *Erasable pens:* black and dark blue. Additional colors if you wish. (Test for permanence—see *Pens and Inks*, page 83.)
- *Super-fine tip, permanent markers:* black and dark blue. Additional colors if you wish. I like Uniball Visions and fine-point Sharpies. (Test for permanence.)
- *Colored markers:* permanent ones, for marking colors on master templates and foundations. (Test for permanence.)
- *Eraser:* a narrow one, like the ones on the ends of pencils, or the ones in a plastic housing that slide down as you use them.
- *Transparent tape:* I prefer Scotch brand in the green box, ¾" wide. Unlike other brands, it doesn't melt under my iron. Test whatever tape you use under your iron. If it melts, reduce the iron temperature.
- *Opaque white paper:* For making master templates. If you're a fan of freezer paper, you can use that.
- *Translucent foundation material:* For making the foundations that you sew fabric onto.

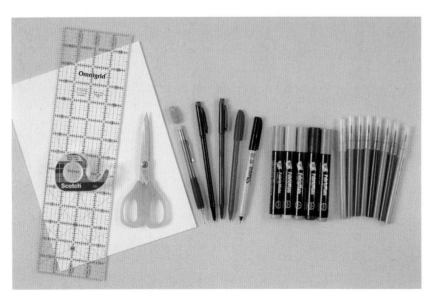

Foundation-Making Tools and Materials

From left to right: Opaque white paper, straightedge, transparent tape, scissors, mechanical pencils, erasable pens, super-fine permanent marker, colored markers.

Drawing Tip

Pencil and pen widths vary, so use the same pencil or pen consistently throughout the drawing process to keep lines and measurements accurate.

Start With the Right Materials

Pens and Inks

Some inkjet printer inks are water-soluble and will run if they get wet. Some laser printer and photocopier toners melt off paper when ironed. Some pens, even though they say they are permanent, still run. Take a minute before you begin to test your materials.

Print and/or write on a test sheet of your foundation material. Cut the sheet in half so printing and/or writing is on both halves. If it's fabric, immerse half the sheet in a sink of warm, soapy water to see if the ink runs or flakes. If it's paper, spray or drip water on it. Now iron the wet half between two pieces of white paper to see if the ink runs or flakes when pressed. Press the dry half between two pieces of white paper with and without steam to see if the heat and/or steam causes the ink or toner to run or flake.

If any ink or toner runs or flakes, but you still want to use it, take these precautions:

- **Ink runs when wet:** Use a dry iron, a wooden presser or a seam roller. If you use a steam iron, be sure it is fully heated before ironing so water doesn't drip out.
- **Toner flakes or melts:** Use a wooden presser or a seam roller. If you use an iron, use the lowest effective iron temperature. Print the pattern on the *back* of the foundation material in mirror-image, then sew and press on the *front* of the foundation. Keep the ironing board clean by covering it with an old dish towel or pillowcase.

Foundation Materials

I prefer translucent foundation material because you can see through it. Traditional methods of paper piecing involve drawing the design on the back of opaque paper and placing fabric on the front. This presents two problems: (1) you can't see what you're doing from the front; and (2) the design on the front is the mirror image of the design on the back, so you have to work in reverse. Translucent foundations solve both these problems: You can see the lines from both sides. Place fabric on the front and sew from the back, and the design will turn out the way you drew it. Translucent foundation also makes the design process easier—it's easy to reverse a spiral simply by turning it over.

There is a wide variety of translucent foundation materials on the market. When you select one for your project, it should have these characteristics:

- You can see the lines from both sides of the material.
- You can mark the design easily on the material—print it, photocopy it or write on it.
- The markings remain permanent on the material. (See *Pens and Inks* on this page.)
- The material holds up to being pressed, steamed, rolled, folded and scrunched through the sewing machine numerous times.
- The material can be easily removed or safely left in without shrinking, clumping, shredding or melting.
- If the material is to be left in, it's light enough to quilt through.

Spiral size should factor into your foundation choice. Paper is fine for small spirals. For large spirals, non-woven tear-away, rinse-away or lightweight Pellon is best, since these are flexible and strong enough to hold up to being folded and passed through the sewing machine many times (a large sheet of paper will warp and tear).

Different Types of Translucent Foundation Material

Top to bottom, left to right: Simply Foundations Translucent Vellum Paper; RinsAway; Solvy (rinse-away) and Tear-Easy from Sulky; Pellon with 1" grid; vellum sheets from Nancy's Notions; Fun-dation non-woven foundation sheets; EQ Printables Foundation Sheets.

DEMONSTRATION

Making a Spiral Foundation

*N*ow that you have your tools and materials, it's time to prepare master templates and foundations. You'll draw, copy or print a master template for each different spiral in your design. After that, you'll trace the master template markings to translucent material for the foundations. Make one foundation for each individual spiral you're going to sew.

Supplies and tools

- Foundation material
- Pen with correction fluid, erasable pen or pencil
- Plain white opaque paper for master template
- Several permanent colored pens
- Transparent tape, pins or stapler
- Translucent foundation materials

1 *Print or Draw the Master Templates (not pictured)*
Draw, copy or print the master template on plain white opaque paper. (Some people like to print them on the dull side of freezer paper so the pieces can be ironed to yardage later for cutting.)

2 *Test the Fit of Assembled Templates*
If you printed or copied templates separately, test that they fit together. Lay them together the way they'll fit in the quilt. If they don't fit exactly, lay them the way they *should* fit.

If there's a gap, put paper behind them to fill the gaps, then draw the line between them where you want it to be and erase or mask the line you don't want (figure A). If the lines overlap, mark the correct line and erase or mask the line you don't want (figure B).

Remember: If it fits on paper, it will fit on cloth. It's as simple as that.

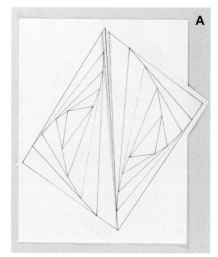

A

How to Assemble Sections of a Template

If you need to assemble sections of a template:

- For paper templates use transparent tape on both edges of the paper front and back.

- For a non-woven fabric, assemble pieces on the sewing machine with a long and wide zigzag stitch at each edge of the two joined sheets or use fabric glue.

Tips for Photocopying and Printing Templates

- If copying a template from a book, the page must be completely flat against the plate so there's no distortion.

- If the template is larger than the copier paper, photocopy the template in sections and assemble the copy (see *How to Assemble Sections of a Template*, above).

- Measure copied or printed templates, since some copy machines and printers may reduce or distort images slightly.

- If you're making more than one photocopy, make all copies from the *same original* on the *same machine* at the *same time*, since different machines can have different reduction/distortion rates.

- Don't make photocopies of photocopies: If the machine is reducing or distorting the copy, copies of copies will become successively more distorted.

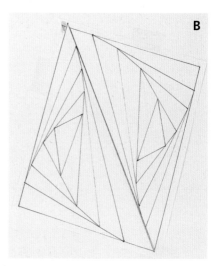

B

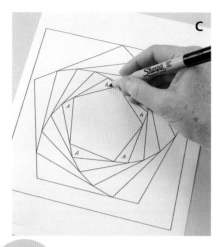

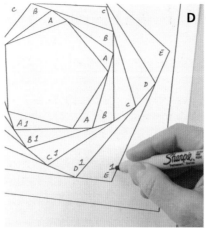

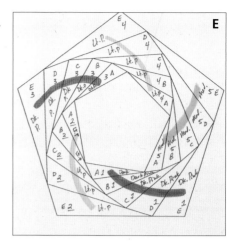

3 Mark the Master Templates

The master template contains the information you'll need to assemble each spiral in fabric. Mark one for each different spiral in your design—different shape or different color—as follows:

Label all the triangles in each ring with a letter, starting with "A" for the ring closest to the center (figure C).

Working from the center out, label all the triangles in each spoke with the same number: "1" for all triangles in the first spoke, "2" for all triangles in the second spoke, and so on (figure D). Each triangle now has a unique number/letter combination that indicates its position in the spiral. (As you get accustomed to working with spirals, you may find that you no longer need the numbers and letters.)

Mark each triangle of each spiral with a permanent colored pen that corresponds to the fabric for that triangle. Draw one continuous line through all the triangles of that color in each spoke to help you see the flow of colors in the design (figure E). If you plan to photocopy the master template to the foundation material, write the names of the colors in the triangles. Don't use numbers—they can get mixed up with the piece numbers.

Template Time-Savers

- If you have exact mirror-image versions of a spiral, there's no need to make two master templates. Copy the markings to the translucent foundation, then flip it over and mark the back side "Front."

- If you have different colorations of the same shape spiral, print or copy the basic spiral and numbers onto the foundation material (and if necessary assemble the sections), then mark the colors by hand.

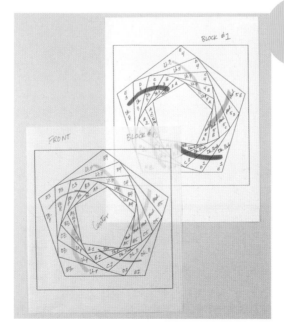

4 Transfer the Master Template Markings to the Foundations

Assemble translucent material to the correct size, if necessary. Tape, pin or staple the foundation material over the master template. Trace all the markings from the master template to the foundation. Repeat this step to make one foundation for each spiral you will sew.

Foundation Choices

*L*isted below are some translucent foundation products I or my students have used successfully for spirals. The list is not comprehensive. I've also listed certain products *not* to use for foundations, and why. See the *Resources* section for ordering information.

Papers

Simple Foundations Translucent Vellum Paper (C&T Publishing)	Can be printed on inkjet or laser printers, also runs through photocopy machines, holds up to wear, tears away easily.
Plain white paper	OK if thin enough to see lines from both sides. Some inks, such as laser printer and photocopier toner, are less visible from the back; stitch without thread or fold along the lines to make them visible from both sides.

Rinse-Away Foundation Products

Fabri-Solvy (Sulky)	Comes in a variety of sizes, so it's good for small or large projects. Follow manufacturer's directions for rinsing away before quilting. Users say it helps to tear away large areas before rinsing.

Leave-In or Remove Foundation Products

EQ Printables Foundation Sheets (Electric Quilt)	Non-woven 8½" × 11" sheets that can be printed in an inkjet or laser printer, but not photocopied. Rather stiff if left in but softens over time; may make quilting more difficult.
Foundation Stuff (George Siciliano)	8½" × 11" that can be printed in an inkjet or laser printer, but not photocopied. Soft yet stable; easy to quilt through.
Tear-Easy (Sulky)	Comes in a variety of sizes, so it's good for small or large projects.

Leave-In Foundation Products

Lightweight Pellon	Comes in a variety of weights and widths, some with 1" grid. Use the lightest weight that is translucent and soft yet stable. Test Pellon with your iron: Too much heat may cause it to shrink. Grid lines and markings may show through light-colored fabrics, so carefully cut it from behind light colors after piecing.
Lightweight muslin or organza	Woven fabrics are the least stable foundations. If you do use one, wash and pre-shrink before using. Iron flat and use a light spray starch or sizing for more stability.

Not Recommended

Mixing foundation types	Different materials may respond to washing, heat and sewing tension differently, and you could end up with blocks that are not the same size.
Vellum paper from the stationery store	OK for designing, but don't use it for sewing. It curls and becomes brittle when ironed. If you do sew with it, cold-press with fingers, a wooden presser or a roller.
Art store tracing paper	Not strong enough to hold up to manipulation. Tears easily and, like vellum, it can curl and become brittle when ironed.
Newsprint	Good for sketching and working out ideas, but not for sewing. It is not translucent and not strong enough to hold up to manipulation.

Calculating Yardage

*Y*ou have to know if you have enough fabric, or how much to buy, right? You could just guess, and that may be OK for small projects. But I have "guess-timated" and then run short and had to go searching all over the Internet for a quarter yard of the fabric because it sold out at my local quilt shop yesterday! I learned my lesson—it's worth doing a bit of math!

Yardage Calculation Chart

Calculate yardage after you have marked your master templates (see *Preparing Foundation*, page 82). The *Yardage Calculation Chart* (pages 146-147) can help you. The chart is primarily designed for solid and non-directional patterns. For "special needs" fabrics, follow the instructions below and in the chart, Insert these special measurements in the line provided at the bottom of the chart.

Fussy-Cutting & Border Prints

For fussy-cutting, count how many copies of a motif you need. Rather than calculate yardage, look at fabric when you are at the store and buy as many repetitions of that motif as you need. Add a couple of extra repetitions for insurance, if you wish. If you prefer not to piece borders, buy at least the length of the border strips you want to cut.

Stripes, Geometrics and Other Directional Prints

Depending on how you intend to cut directional prints, you may need up to three times the amount of fabric calculated with the *Yardage Calculation Chart*. Your best bet is to lay out templates on paper, a cutting mat or the fabric itself and physically measure the amount of fabric needed for cutting. If you have many pieces, lay out a portion of them and then multiply the result.

How to Use the *Yardage Calculation Chart* (Appendix 1, page 146)

- Make one copy of Part 1 and Part 2 of the chart for each fabric in your design. Tape the two parts together into one sheet.

- Where the chart asks for measurements, measure the pieces on the master template. The chart will tell you when and what to add, multiply and divide. Work through the chart line by line in order.

- Fill out one complete chart for each fabric.

- Take all the charts with you when buying fabric.

- When you have chosen the fabric, staple a swatch of the fabric to the chart for reference.

- The calculations in the chart build in a proportionate amount of extra fabric, but if you feel you need more for comfort, add extra. (The chart explains the underlying assumptions on which the calculations are based if you want to understand where the numbers come from.)

- There is a line at the bottom to add in extra yardage for fussy-cutting and/or directional fabrics.

Cutting Fabric for Spirals

*O*ne of the big advantages of foundation piecing is that fabric does not have to be cut accurately. Seam allowances (as long as they are wide enough) are not critical because you don't line pieces up edge-to-edge. Choose the cutting method that best suits your working style and fabric needs.

Template Method

In the template method of cutting, you cut up the master template after marking the translucent foundations, then use the pieces of the master template as templates for cutting fabric to the correct size and shape. The template method is the best method for Point-to-Point spirals because these spirals have such wide variation in the sizes of triangles. It can, however, be used for any type of spiral. It's a

A Note About Fabrics

Printed fabrics are printed on one side and the dyes do not go through to the back side, so there is a "right" side and a "wrong" side. Always cut with both templates and fabric right side up. Since most triangles are directional, reversing either the template or the fabric may result in triangles that are backwards.

Through-dyed fabrics such as batiks and hand-dyes are the same color on both sides because the fabric is immersed in dye. Since there is no wrong side, if you happen to cut a piece backwards you can just flip it over. Even so, it's best to get in the habit of always placing templates and fabric face up.

more efficient use of fabric than the strip method, so use the template method if yardage is tight.

Templates for this method are pieces of the master template, so they have no seam allowances. When laying out templates for cutting be sure to add ¼" or more seam allowance to all sides. Be generous. You can always trim down later, but too small means wasted time and fabric.

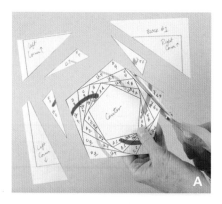

1 Cut up the Master Template

After you have prepared all the translucent foundations, cut up the master template precisely along the seam lines (figure A). Group the cut pieces by fabric. Work on only one spiral at a time—don't mix spirals.

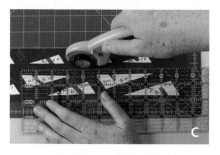

2 Arrange the Template Pieces

Spread the fabric face-up on the cutting surface. Arrange templates face-up on the fabric with ¾" between templates to allow a ⅜" seam allowance on each piece. I think of this as a generous ¼". Even more is better on large pieces. Use double-sided tape to hold templates in place (figure B).

3 Cut the Fabric

Use scissors or a rotary cutter to cut in the spaces between the templates—not along the edges of the paper. Cut a ¼" seam allowance along the base edge of the triangles (figures C1 and C2, opposite page) and ¼" or more seam allowance on the other sides. Cut the largest pieces and work down to the smallest. For smaller pieces, cut in strips, then cut down to individual pieces (figure C and D).

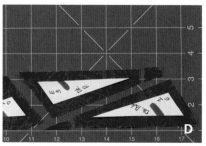

Leave the templates on each piece of fabric for identification. Group the cut pieces by ring from smallest (first to be sewn) to largest (last to be sewn).

Strip Method

In the strip method of cutting, you cut rectangular strips of fabric, which you trim down to triangles after sewing them to the foundation. The strip method works best with Nesting, Pinwheel and Baravelle spirals, because the triangles in these spirals tend to be rather uniform in height. While it does waste a certain amount of fabric, many quilters find that the time saved is worth the fabric wasted. A big advantage of this method is that if you have mirror-image spirals or are changing directions in a spiral, you don't have to worry about orientation—the rectangle will fit either a "right" or a "left" triangle. This is the best method for working with very small pieces of fabric, because you have more fabric to handle. It's also best for directional fabrics. With the strip method, you can cut fabric as you work if you wish, eliminating the risk of lost pieces and the need for careful organizing.

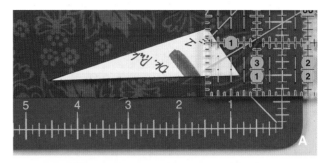

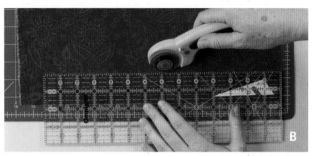

1 *Calculate the Strip Length*

Measure the height of the triangles you're going to cut and add ¾". This is the width of the strips (figure A). Measure the length of the triangles and add ¾" (L+¾"). Count how many triangles of this size you will cut from this fabric. Multiply the triangle length plus ¾" by the number of triangles. This tells you how many inches of strip you need.

L + ¾"		# of Triangles		Total Strip Length
_____	×	_____	=	_____

2 *Cut the Strips*

Cut enough strips of fabric to give you the total length needed. You can cut as many strips as you need all at once for the total strip length (figure B). Or, cut strips as you work.

3 *Cut the Pieces From the Strips*

Cut strips down into rectangles for each triangle (remember, length + ¾"). You can do this all at once before sewing the spiral, or cut strips down into rectangles as you work. Place the base edge along a straight edge of fabric. Remember, the base edge is not always the longest side of the triangle (figures C1 and C2).

Leave the templates on each piece of fabric for identification. Group the cut pieces by ring from smallest (first to be sewn) to largest (last to be sewn).

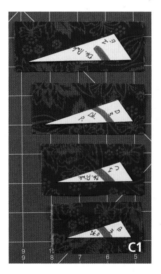

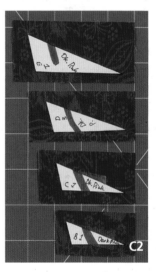

Pay Attention to the Base

Be aware that the longest side of a triangle is not always its base. In Type A triangles (figure C1), the longest side is the base, but in Type B triangles (figure C2), the middle-length side is the base. (See *All About Triangles*, page 11). Having a straight, even ¼"-seam allowance on the base edge will help you sew your spiral quickly and easily. It isn't essential to place the base edge on-grain, but if you can, the fabric will be more stable when you sew.

Preparing the Sewing Machine

Tension: Use a normal tension that lets the threads cross between the layers of fabric, not on the back or the front. If you're using removable foundation, don't use a loose tension setting, because the threads will be even looser when the thickness of the foundation is gone.

Stitch Length: If you use removable foundations, use the smallest stitch you can while still being able to get the tip of a seam ripper under a single stitch. I use about twenty stitches to the inch. Depending on your sewing machine, this is around a 1.2 or 1.4 stitch length. The more stitches per inch, the more perforations in the foundation, and the easier it is to remove. If you use leave-in foundation, you can use longer stitches.

Needle: Have several needles on hand, as sewing through paper can dull needles more quickly than sewing just fabric. A 70/10 needle seems to be the favorite among my students.

Thread: Use fine cotton or silk thread that will add a minimum of bulk to the seam—40 or 50 weight or lingerie thread is good. Spend the money for good quality, strong thread. Use a color that will blend into the fabric. Since you will be stitching with the foundation side up, the needle thread will be against the foundation. Try to use a color other than white in the needle (unless you're sewing white fabric) so your stitching is easier to see against the foundation.

Foot: Use a foot with a slot in the center that can align with the stitching line on the foundation. (Some people prefer an open-toe foot, as it allows a wider view of the stitching area.)

Seam Roller

A seam roller is one of my favorite tools. It makes a firm, clean fold, it is quick and easy to use right at the sewing machine, simple to carry, cool to use and energy efficient. Get one with a barrel-shaped (not cylindrical) roller.

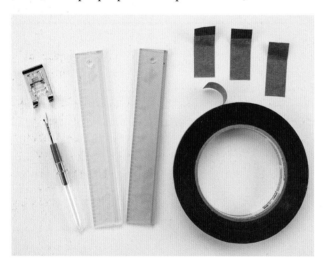

Tools for Sewing

Masking or painter's tape, ¾- to 1-inch wide (alternative to pins); Add-a-Quarter or Add-an-Eighth Tool; seam ripper; pins; center-slot foot; pins (not shown).

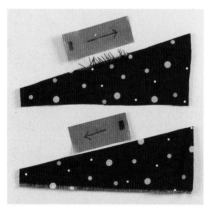

Tape Removal

When you remove tape from a bias-cut edge, pull toward the narrow tip of the triangle to avoid fraying the raw edges. I prefer tape instead of pins for holding fabric when working with a foundation. Cut 2- to 3-inch lengths and fold under ¼" on one end for an easy-to-grasp tab.

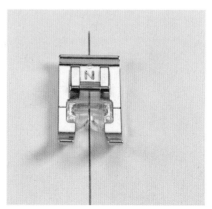

Positioning, Pinning and Taping

*H*ow you position and pin fabric is crucial for successful spirals. When pinning fabric to the foundation, double-check that the piece of fabric you're going to sew is the right size to cover the area of the foundation it's intended for, including seam allowance. Use proper pinning technique (see *How NOT to Pin* below).

Most of the time, you will have done a "next step" trim (see *Trimming and Pressing Seams*, page 93), so simply align the edge of the fabric with the trimmed edge of the previous ring, then tape or pin the fabric in place. If not, follow the steps on this page.

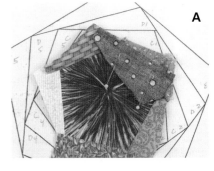

A

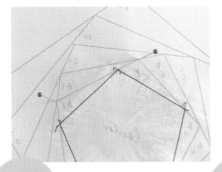

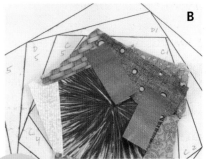

B

1 *Mark Seam Ends With Pins*
From the foundation side, stick the pins through the ends of the seam line to mark them. Flip to the front side.

2 *Align the Fabric Pieces*
Turn the piece of fabric you are about to sew face down and fold back the seam allowance on the base edge. (This is the long side on Type A triangles, or the medium side on Type B triangles—see page 11.) Align the folded edge with the pins sticking through the foundation, leaving ¼" beyond each pin. (Measure from the tip if you're working with Type B triangles, so the fabric reaches over the extended peak.)

3 *Tape or Pin*
Tape or pin the fabric in place as follows, staying clear of the seam line you are about to sew:

To pin, slide pins sideways through the new fabric and a layer of already-sewn fabric beneath it. Avoid pinning through the foundation unless you must, because it bends (figure A).

To tape, apply tape in the same position you would apply pins, avoiding seam lines (figure B).

How NOT to Pin
Never stick the pin straight in and then lean it sideways to bring it back up through the fabric and foundation. The layers will shift and warp; seams and points won't align.

Stitching Techniques

Basic Stitching Tips

Follow these tips as you stitch:

- After positioning the fabric on the front of the foundation, turn it over and stitch along the seam line on the back. This lets you see and stitch the seam line precisely.
- Begin and end stitching two or three stitches beyond the ends of the seam line; don't backstitch at the beginning and end. The bulk of the backstitching will complicate joining blocks and quilting.
- If the lines on the foundation are wider than the thread, decide before you start sewing whether you will stitch on the inside edge or the outside edge of the line, and stick with it through the whole quilt. This will keep your points sharp and all your blocks the same size.
- Don't try to correct a mistake by adjusting other seam lines around it. Remove it and re-stitch.

How to Cross Intersections

As you add rings to the spiral, you will cross the previously sewn corners of the preceding ring of triangles. It's very important that you cross these intersections correctly, so the corners of the triangles meet precisely and the edges of the spokes are smooth. Pay close attention to the photos at right so you know what to do and what to avoid.

Handling Excess Bulk at Points

As the layers of fabric grow, the areas around narrow points will become bulky. The bulk may cause the fabric to slip out from under the sewing machine foot, causing the layers of fabric to slip out of alignment or seam lines to become crooked. There are several solutions:

- Start sewing at the bulkiest part of the seam so the foot slides off the bulk instead of onto it.
- Stitch slowly and hold the fabric under the foot with the tip of a seam ripper.
- Lighten the pressure on the foot. Also some newer sewing machines have a sensor that will do this automatically. Some sewing machine feet have a button you can press to stabilize the foot over thick areas to prevent slipping.

Stitch Along the Seam Line
Once the fabric is pinned or taped to the front of the foundation, turn it over and stitch along the seam line on the back of the foundation.

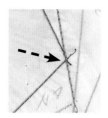 

Touch the Previous Intersection
Stitch so that the needle/thread just touches the inside of the threads of the previous intersection.

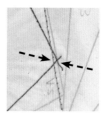 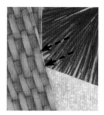

Don't Stitch Inside the Previous Intersection
If you stitch inside the intersection of stitching lines, the corners of the triangles will not meet. This will also cut off the tip of the triangle in the next ring, causing an uneven edge on the spoke.

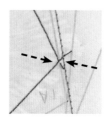 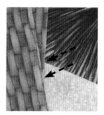

Don't Stitch Outside the Previous Intersection
If you stitch outside the intersection of stitching lines, the triangles will overlap, and the triangles will not meet in the next ring.

Trimming and Pressing Seams

Wherever a light fabric lies over a dark fabric, trim the seam allowance of the light fabric slightly wider than the dark fabric. This prevents the dark fabric from showing through the light fabric.

Trim All Seam Allowances

Every time you finish sewing a piece of fabric, flip the fabric into place and make sure it's positioned correctly, including adequate seam allowances. Then fold the fabric and foundation back and trim the seam allowance to ¼" (at tips, taper the seam allowance from ¼" to ⅛"; on very small pieces trim the entire seam allowance to ⅛").

Always Press Your Seams

After trimming a seam, flip the fabric right-side up into position and press with an iron or seam roller. Be sure the fold falls precisely at the seam line.

After pressing, pin or tape the loose edge of the fabric to the foundation, avoiding seam lines. This prevents the fold of the fabric from slipping when the next piece of fabric is sewn over it. Always press the flipped fabric before sewing the next piece of fabric over it.

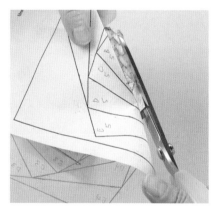

Ensure Perfect Seams

Gently pull the fabric completely back from the seam line so that the fold line falls precisely at the seam line. This is critical for accurate points and smooth edges on the spokes (above, right). If the fabric folds over the seam line, the tip of the triangle will be blunt, the edge of the spoke will be jagged, and the next ring of triangles will not align properly (right).

Next Step Trim

After you have sewn and pressed an entire ring, do a "next step" trim as shown below. When you position the fabric for the next ring, you'll be able to simply align it along this trimmed edge.

 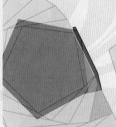 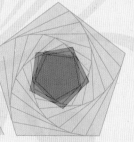

Trimming Tools

You can trim with scissors (above, top), or with an Add-a-Quarter or Add-an-Eighth tool (above, bottom left and right). If you use the Add-a-Quarter, angle it to taper from ¼" to ⅛" at narrow tips. Since you can't see the fabric under the foundation, be careful to fold the fabric completely back from the seam to avoid cutting off the fabric by mistake.

1. Place the spiral face-down on cutting mat. Highlight the line you'll sew for the next ring of triangles.

2. Fold the foundation back on the highlighted seam line for the next ring (yellow line). Trim to ¼" beyond fold.

3. Repeat for each triangle around the ring.

Sewing Nesting and Baravelle Spirals

*A*ll spirals are constructed by sewing rings of triangles from center to edge, although the order in which you sew the triangles within the rings of Nesting and Baravelle spirals is different from Pinwheel and Point-to-Point spirals. However, the first step for all spirals setting the center. With Nesting and Baravelle spirals, you can sew more than one triangle at the same time as long as they are not next to each other in the ring. This is because the triangle in the next ring completely covers the crossover of the triangles in the previous ring, hiding the direction of the crossover.

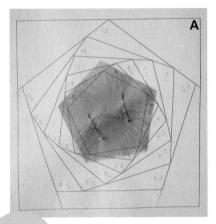
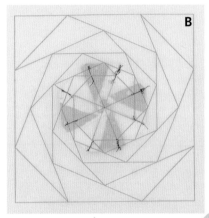
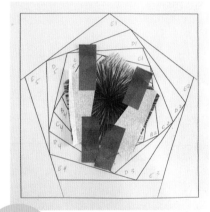

1 Set the Center (Applies to All Spiral Types)

Place the center fabric face down on the table, then position the foundation over it so that the edges overlap the first ring of seam lines by at least ¼" (A).

If the center is pieced, place the seam lines exactly over the corresponding seam lines in the center of the foundation (B). Make sure the colors in the center are in the correct colored areas on the foundation. Pin, tape or baste the center securely into place.

2 Ring A (First Ring Around Center), Even-Numbered Triangles

Position the fabric for the even-numbered triangles face down on the front of the foundation. Be sure to place the correct colors in the correct positions. Pin or tape into position.

3 Stitch Along the Seam Line

Turn the foundation over and stitch from the back along the seam line for each triangle. If the excess fabric for one triangle overlaps the seam line of another, fold it out of the way while stitching.

Take a Break!

Sewing spirals requires concentration. You will work faster and with fewer mistakes if you work in an environment without distractions. Try to work at times when you are not tired, and take breaks often to refresh yourself and stay alert.

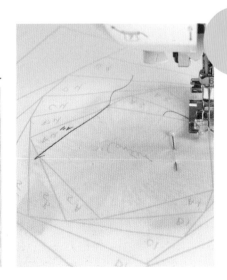

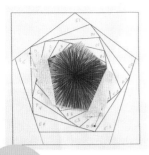

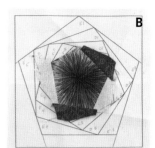

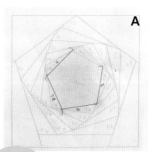

A

B

4 Trim, Press and Pin

Trim seam allowances. Flip fabric right-side up and press back from seam lines. (See pressing instructions on page 104.) Pin or tape loose edges of fabric into position.

5 Ring A, Odd-Numbered Triangles

Position the fabric for the odd-numbered triangles face down on the front of the foundation. If the spiral has an uneven number of sides, leave off the last triangle. Pin or tape.

6 Stitch, Trim, Press and Pin
Repeat steps 3 and 4.

7 Ring A, Last Triangle

If the spiral has an uneven number of sides, position the fabric for the last triangle face down on the front of the foundation. Pin or tape.

8 Stitch, Trim, Press and Pin

Repeat steps 3 and 4, then do a "Next Step Trim" (page 93).

9 Ring B Through Outer Ring

Repeat the steps above for each ring of triangles, moving out from the center, until you reach the edge of the foundation. Carefully follow the color placements marked on the foundation. As you add rings to the spiral, you will see the spokes grow.

If your spiral is set in a block with background around it, finish by adding the background fabric around the spiral.

When you complete the block, leave at least ¼" of fabric beyond the outer line of the foundation for a seam allowance when joining blocks. Baste the edges of the fabric to the edges of the foundation. Do not remove the foundation.

Sewing Pinwheel and Point-to-Point Spirals

*I*n Pinwheel and Point-to-Point spirals, each triangle overlaps the triangle next to it. So, the triangles must be pinned and sewn one at a time in order around the ring. Pinwheel and Point-to-Point spirals usually require partial seam piecing—the tip of the first triangle is left unsewn until the last triangle is in place.

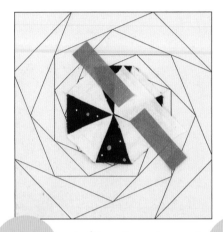

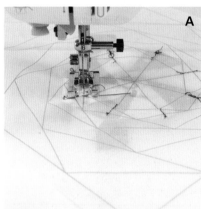
A

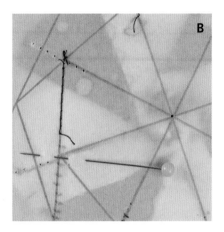
B

1 *Ring A (First Ring Around Center), First Triangle*
Set the center (step 1, page 94). Position the fabric for the first triangle face down on the front of the foundation. Pin or tape into position.

2 *Stitch the Partial Seam*
Turn the foundation over and stitch from the back part way along the seam line from the wide end toward the narrow tip (figure A). Stop at least ¼" before the seam line of the last triangle. (The pin in figure B indicates where the last seam line meets the first seam line.) This is the partial seam. You'll come back and finish it later.

3 *Trim, Press and Pin*
Trim the seam allowance in the sewn section. Flip the fabric right-side up and press back from the seam line. Also press the seam line on the unsewn tip of the triangle. Pin or tape the loose edge of fabric into position on the foundation. Pin the loose tip out of the way.

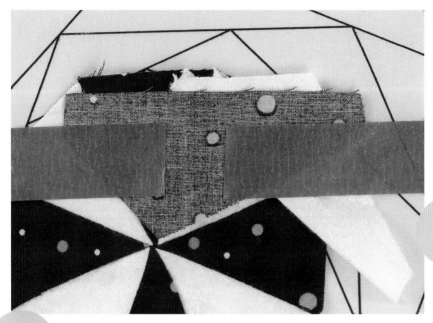

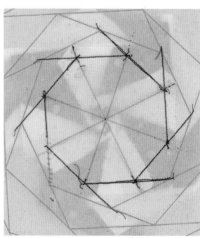

5 Stitch the Entire Seam
Turn the foundation over and stitch on the back all the way along the seam line.

4 Ring A, Second Triangle
Work around the ring in order, one triangle at a time. The next triangle is always the one that crosses the shortest side of the previously sewn triangle. Position the fabric face-down on the front of the foundation. Pin or tape into position.

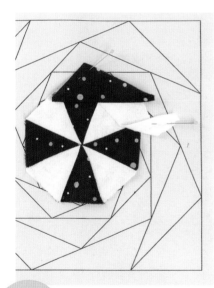

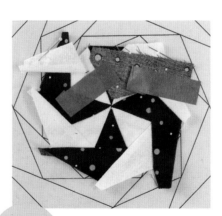

6 Trim, Press and Pin
Trim the seam allowance. Flip the fabric right-side up and press back from the seam line. Pin or tape the loose edge of the fabric into position on the foundation.

7 Complete the Spiral
Continue adding triangles, working around the ring in order, until the spiral is complete.

Foundation Back
This photo shows the back of the foundation after all triangles of the ring are sewn in place. The red marks show the section of the first seam that remains to be sewn.

Method 1:

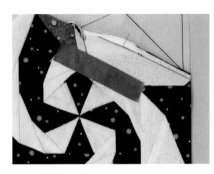

A: Locate the seam that crosses the short side of the first triangle.

B: Tear it free from the foundation. Unfold the first triangle so it lays flat with the seam open and face down. Align the pressed seam line on the unsewn portion of the fabric with the seam line on the foundation. Pin or tape into position.

C: Turn to the foundation side and finish stitching the seam. Put a piece of transparent tape over the tear in the foundation.

D: Return the first triangle to its position. Pin the torn-out seam precisely back over its seam line through the transparent tape. Begin the next ring of triangles at a different spoke in order to hold the loose seam in place.

8 *Ring A, Closing the First Triangle (Partial Seam)*
Position and sew the loose tip of the first triangle over the last triangle, using one of the following methods:

Method 2:

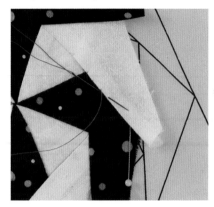

Lay the pressed edge of the first triangle along its seam line. Blind-stitch in place by hand or top-stitch by machine with a narrow zigzag stitch.

Method 3:

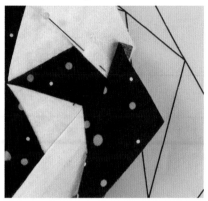

Lay the pressed edge of the first triangle along its seam line. Pin it in place. Start sewing the next ring of triangles at a different spoke so the loose tip has a complete seam line above it holding it in place. When you've completed the whole spiral, go back and close all the open edges by hand, or just quilt over them.

9 *Rings B Through Outer Ring*
Repeat the steps above for each ring of triangles, moving out from the center, until you reach the edge of the foundation. Carefully follow the color placements marked on the foundation. As you add rings to the spiral, you'll see the spokes grow.

If your spiral is set in a block with background around it, finish by adding the background fabric around the spiral.

When you complete the block, leave at least ¼" of fabric beyond the outer line of the foundation for a seam allowance when joining blocks. Baste the edges of the fabric to the edges of the foundation. Do not remove the foundation.

Sewing Sawtooth Edges (Pinwheel Spirals)

Sawtooth edges happen when you sew over the tips of triangles of a Pinwheel spiral, making them blunt. (See *Pinwheel With Sawtooth Edges*, page 44, for a full explanation.) This can be an interesting design element, or, in some cases, it can help you avoid sewing partial seams. Before beginning, familiarize yourself with the instructions for sewing Pinwheel and Point-to-Point spirals on page 96.

One Sawtooth Edge or Avoiding a Partial Seam

Place the blunt tip between the triangles of *contrasting* colors for a sawtooth edge. Place the blunt tip between the triangles of the *same* color (preferably a dark color or a busy print) to hide it.

A: Begin each ring with the triangle that will have the blunt tip. Instead of leaving the first triangle partially unsewn, sew all the way to the tip.

B: As you work around the ring, the next triangle is always the one that crosses the increment side of the previous triangle. (This is the same direction as sewing Pinwheel and Point-to-Point spirals.) Sew the second through the last triangles around the ring.

C: Sew the last triangle over the tip of the first triangle, creating the blunt tip or sawtooth. There will be no partial seam to close at the end.

Sew all the rings the same way, always beginning at the same spoke so the blunt tips align along the edge.

All-But-One Sawtooth Edges

D: Begin each ring with the triangle whose shortest side will be on the smooth edge. Instead of leaving the first triangle partially unsewn, sew all the way to the tip.

E: As you work around the ring, the next triangle is always the one that crosses the *tip* of the previous triangle. (This is the opposite direction from sewing Pinwheel and Point-to-Point spirals, and from the instructions for a single sawtooth edge.)

F: Sew the second through the last triangles around the ring. Extend the seam lines of all the triangles over the tips of the previous triangles. The last triangle will cross the shortest side of the first triangle, creating the smooth spoke. There will be no partial seam to close at the end.

Sew all the rings the same way, always beginning at the same spoke.

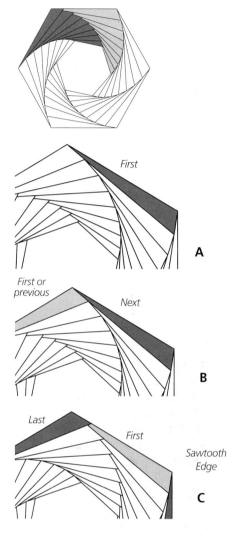

First

A

First or previous · Next

B

Last · First · Sawtooth Edge

C

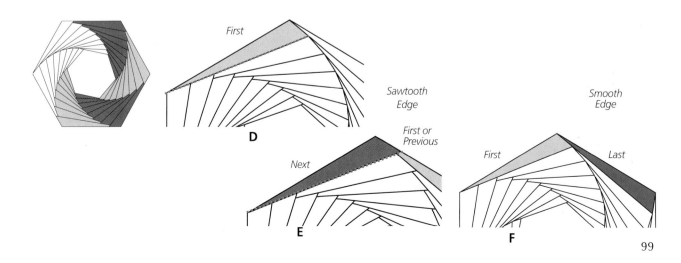

First · Sawtooth Edge

D

Next · First or Previous · Sawtooth Edge

E

Smooth Edge · First · Last

F

Sawtooth Edges *continued*

All Sawtooth Edges

Follow the instructions for sewing Pinwheel and Point-to-Point spirals, but go in the opposite direction so you're crossing tips of triangles, not short sides. Leave the partial seam of the first triangle open on the increment side of the triangle. Working around the ring, the next triangle will always be the one that crosses the tip of the previous triangle. Finish by closing the partial seam.

More Than One—But Not All—Sawtooth Edges

It's possible to create more than one sawtooth edge in a spiral simply by changing the order you sew the triangles. Explore the possibilities. *Hint:* Always sew the blunt tip triangles first.

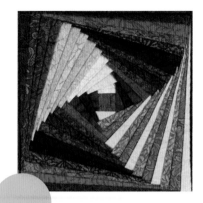

Detail, Florida 2007
page 44

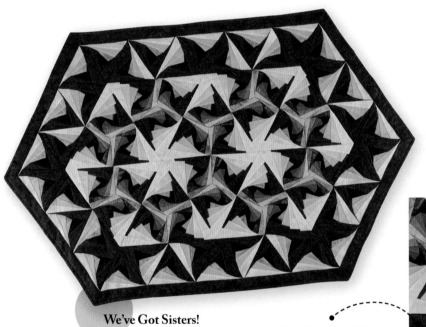

We've Got Sisters!
33½" × 22"
Designed, pieced and quilted by
MaryAnn Olmstead

Hiding and Highlighting Sawtooth Edges

In this table runner, sawtooth edges are highlighted between yellow and green spokes as a design element, and are hidden between adjacent green spokes in the border for easier construction.

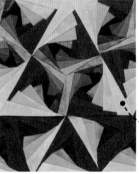

Sawtooth edges as a design element at edges of yellow spokes

Partial seams avoided here, between dark green spokes

Fixing Mistakes

Problem: I have to rip out and re-sew a seam.

Here is my preferred method for seam removal in paper piecing: Working on the foundation side, slip the tip of the seam ripper under every fourth stitch and cut it. Turn to the front and pull on the top thread. The seam will pop out like a zipper. Use a piece of tape to pick up bits of thread.

When you re-stitch, use the exact same stitch length as the first time. Place the needle precisely in the first hole leftover from the previous stitching and re-stitch in the holes left from the previous stitching. Or, after removing the stitching, place a strip of transparent tape over the seam line before re-stitching. Either method avoids over-perforating the line so the foundation doesn't fall apart.

Problem: My spoke has jagged edges.

Reason #1: The fabric is not pressed completely back from the seam. (This is the most common reason.)

Solution: When pressing each piece, pull the fabric all the way back from the seam. Pin or tape it to anchor it until the next piece is sewn over it. If you've already sewn over it, open up the seam of the triangle beyond it, pull the slack out, and re-stitch the opened seam by hand. (See *Trimming and Pressing Seams*, page 93.)

Reason #2: If you're sewing a Pinwheel spiral, and this is happening on every triangle, you're sewing the triangles in the wrong order—after each triangle you are sewing the next triangle over the *point* of the previous triangle. (Note: If you are making sawtooth edges, this is the correct order.)

Solution: Review the instructions for sewing Pinwheel spirals (page 96). Be sure to sew in the correct order—the next triangle should cross the shortest side of the previous triangle.

Reason #3: If you're sewing a Pinwheel spiral, and you're cutting off only the last point, you are forgetting to leave open the partial seam of the first triangle.

Solution: Review the instructions for beginning and ending with a partial seam in Pinwheel and Point-to-Point spirals (page 96).

Problem: The tip of one or all of my triangles is blunt.

This is actually the same problem as jagged edges, above.

Problem: The points of the triangles don't meet (Nesting and Baravelle Spirals).

Reason: You sewed too far inside the seam lines of the crossover.

Solution: Re-sew the seam, making sure to stitch precisely at the crossover. (See *Stitching Techniques*, page 92.) Remove the previous line of stitching.

Problem: The piece of fabric is too short.

Reason #1: If you're sewing Type B triangles (see page 11), it is not the longest side of the triangle but the medium side of the triangle that you sew along. It's easy to accidentally place the triangle too far down the seam line, leaving too little fabric to cover the extending short side.

Solution: Always position the fabric at the tip of the triangle first extending ¼" beyond it, so the remaining length of the fabric reaches over the rest of the triangle. Either remove the fabric and re-sew it farther up or sew on an extension.

Reason #2: You cut the piece too small.

Solution: Either re-cut and re-sew a longer piece of fabric or sew on an extension.

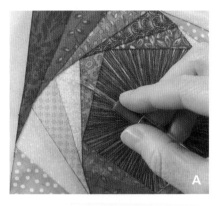

Problem: I accidentally cut off the triangle instead of the seam allowance.

Reason: You're not yet familiar with the mechanics of sewing and trimming the triangles, and accidentally caught the wrong part of the triangle in the rotary cutter or scissors.

Solution: First, scream! Next, take a deep breath. Now remove the shred of leftover triangle, re-cut the piece and re-sew. You can avoid having to remove the seam line if you trim the cut-off triangle precisely at the seam line and pull it out, then place the seam line for the new piece so it just touches the inward side of the old line of stitching.

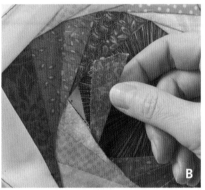

Problem: Raw edges are exposed.

Reason #1: If you're sewing a Point-to-Point or Pinwheel spiral, you may be sewing the triangles in the wrong order—after each triangle you're sewing the next triangle over the *point* of the previous triangle instead of the shortest side.

Solution: Review the instructions for sewing Pinwheel spirals (page 96). Be sure to sew in the correct order—the next triangle should cross the shortest side of the previous triangle.

Reason #2: The piece of fabric is too short.

Problem: The piece is completely sewn in but I want to change it.

Solution:

Use a seam ripper to carefully undo all the seams around the offending piece and slip it out (figure A). Slip the old piece out (figure B). Using the old piece as a template, cut a piece of the new fabric large enough to replace the offending piece (figure C). Press under a seam allowance on the side that will be the inward edge of the triangle. Slide in the new piece with the pressed edge toward the center of the spiral. Use the tip of the seam ripper to ease it into place. Blind-stitch around the edges of the new triangle (stitches are visible in the figure D to show placement).

Joining Blocks

Leave in the Paper!

If you're using paper foundations, hopefully, you have left the foundations attached until now. This makes it easy to join blocks—just line up the corners and the outside lines of the foundations, then sew on the lines.

Pinning

A: Working from the side you will sew from, stick a pin straight through both blocks. Put it precisely through any points you want to match.

B: Pinch the fabric/foundations together on the shaft of the pin.

C: Stick another pin diagonally and almost flat through all the pinned layers, entering the fabric precisely at the base of the up-and-down pin. Lean it over just barely enough to bring it back up through the fabric as far from the entry point as possible. The first pin prevents the layers from shifting.

Remove the first pin. When you sew, put the needle down precisely at the entry point of the second pin (remove it just before you take the stitch) and the points will match.

"Y" Seams

Some people find "Y" seams difficult. This is because fabric stretches and match-up points may not be precise. Don't let "Y" seams scare you. Simply match corner points on the foundations, following the instructions for pinning blocks together (above), then sew precisely to the ends of each of the three intersecting seam lines on the foundations.

Bulky Seams and Seam Allowances

There's really no way to avoid bulky seams in spirals—they are a natural product of piling up layers of fabric at the tips of the triangles.

When you join adjacent spirals, same-direction spirals place the bulkiest part of one spiral at the least bulky point of the adjoining spiral. Mirror image spirals do exactly the opposite: They place the bulkiest parts of both spirals right next to each other. There is no way to avoid this. It helps a bit to try to remove as much foundation as you can from bulky areas, even if you're leaving in the foundation.

I allow seam allowances to fall in the direction they naturally lean, letting the areas of more bulk lie over areas of less bulk. At corners, this often means seam allowances naturally fall into a "pinwheel" arrangement—all the seams go in the same direction around the central point. Sometimes in the middle of a long seam the seam allowance will need to change direction. Where this happens, I press carefully on the front side to flatten a potential tuck or twist in the seam, but avoid clipping the underlying seam allowance unless absolutely necessary.

Finishing the Quilt Top

Removing the Foundations

Part of the decision about whether you would leave in your foundation or remove it was made at the time you selected your foundation—did you choose a removable or a leave-in foundation?

If you used a removable foundation, tear it out only after you have sewn the sections of your quilt that lie beyond the edges of the foundation, since even the outer lines of the foundation are seam lines.

Paper foundations should always be removed unless the quilt will never be washed and you want the stiffness. When removing paper foundations, the stitching lines act as perforations. Pulling paper strips toward the narrow points seems to make the points a bit easier to remove. By nature, spirals have many points where tiny bits of paper can lodge. Some people leave these small bits of paper, but they usually occur where there is already a lot of bulk, so they may have an impact on quilting. I use a pair of tweezers to remove them.

For rinse-away foundations, follow the manufacturer's instructions for removal. Some people like to tear away larger areas of rinse-away foundation before wetting it. After rinsing the foundation, roll your quilt top in an old towel and stand on it to squeeze out excess moisture. Never wring your pieced work!

With non-woven tear-away foundation you have the option to leave it in or remove it. Even if they're somewhat stiff, they usually soften up when wetted or with use.

A leave-in foundation such as lightweight Pellon stays in unless you decide to cut it out. When cutting, be *very* careful to avoid cutting the front of the quilt or seam allowances! I have hand-quilted through lightweight Pellon foundations with no difficulty. You should cut it out if any foundation markings show through light-colored fabrics.

Pressing

With the top assembled and the foundation removed, give your quilt a thorough overall pressing. At this stage, I find the press cloth and padded ironing board particularly useful, and I use steam liberally because it helps to tame bulky areas. (See *Trimming and Pressing Seams*, page 95.)

Quilting

Whether you hand-quilt or machine-quilt your spiral quilt will depend a great deal on how small the pieces are: Smaller pieces mean more seams, and more seams mean more layers of fabric. Also, if you used a leave-in foundation, is it light enough to hand-quilt through?

I hand-quilted my quilts *City Tears to Country Skies* (page 130), *Exploding Spiral* (page 112) and *Infinite Rainbow* (page 128)—all of which were pieced on lightweight Pellon that I left in. On the other hand, Micki Wiersma's quilts *Enjoy the Journey* (page 132) and *Over the Rainbow* (page 132) had so many small pieces that her machine quilter broke three needles while quilting them!

The thickness of your piecing will also have an impact on the type of thread you use—if the piecing is quite dense, use a strong thread.

Take your time to audition a variety of thread colors until you find one (or more) that best suits your design. Sometimes it isn't the one you think is the obvious choice.

As for quilting designs, the spirals themselves are such strong design elements they should be the guiding force. Here are some suggestions to get you thinking (not necessarily to be used all at once!):

- Follow the curves of the spokes.
- Follow the shape of the triangles that form spokes.
- Contain different textures within different spokes.
- Quilt lightly or not at all over the spokes, then quilt heavily in background areas to make the spokes stand out more.
- Echo the spiral theme in non-spiral areas of your quilt.
- Draw out motifs from the fabrics for quilting designs. (See *Majestic Mandalai*, page 140, for a particularly spectacular use of this concept.)

Binding

These are instructions for a standard ½-inch, double-ply binding sometimes called a French binding.

1

Measure each side of your quilt. Add the measurements together to get the total length of binding that you'll need. Add at least 8" to this measurement, for insurance.

2

From the binding fabric, cut enough strips 2½" wide to get the total length of binding needed, plus an additional 2½" of length for each strip. If your quilt has only straight sides, you can cut these strips on the grain. If there are any curves, cut them on the bias (45-degree angle across your fabric).

3

Trim the ends of all the strips at a 45-degree angle, all in the same direction. (This is why you added the extra 2½" in the previous step). Join all the strips end-to-end to make one continuous strip. Press the seams open.

4

Press the strip in half lengthwise with the right side of the fabric on the outside. If you haven't already done so, square up the edges of your quilt.

5

Starting in the middle of a side, place the binding strip on the front of the quilt with the raw edges aligned at the raw edge of the quilt. The folded edge of the binding will face toward the center of the quilt. Pin, leaving about 6" loose at the starting end. Place the last pin exactly ¼" before you reach the first corner of the quilt.

6

Using a ¼" seam, sew from the first pin (leave 6" loose at the starting end) to the corner. Stop exactly ¼" from the first corner and backstitch. Remove the quilt from the sewing machine.

7

Make a mitered corner: Position the quilt on the table in front of you so that the side you just sewed runs from left to right. Fold the binding strip up (away from you) right at the stitch where you stopped sewing; the raw edge is now in a straight line with the side of the quilt that you will sew next. Fold the binding straight down, matching the fold with the raw edge on the side where you just sewed the binding. Align the raw edge of the binding with the raw edge of the side you are about to sew. Pin from this corner to the next corner.

8

Stitch the binding all the way along the new side, and stop exactly ¼" before you reach the corner.

9

Repeat Steps 7 and 8 until you have turned all the corners. When you sew the last side, stop stitching about 8" before the starting point.

10

Unfold both ends of the binding. Lay the open ends face-down on the quilt, aligned with the edge. The finishing end should be underneath the starting end. Use a ruler and pencil to mark where the starting edge lands on the finishing end.

11

Fold back the starting end. With the ruler, mark another line on the finishing end ½" toward the starting end, so that you are *adding* ½" to the marked length on the finishing end. Double-check that you have marked in the right direction. Trim the finishing end on the second line. The starting end and the finishing end now overlap by ½", or two ¼" seam allowances.

12

Pin both ends right sides together and sew them together with a ¼" seam allowance. Press the seam open.

13

Re-fold the binding and finish sewing it to the edge of the quilt.

14

Flip the folded edge of the binding to the back side of the quilt and hand-stitch over the seam line. When you reach a mitered corner, fold it over the corner so that the diagonal fold on the back is on the opposite side from the diagonal fold on the front. (This distributes the bulk evenly.)

Zowie! Powie!
49½" × 49½"

Designed by RaNae Merrill
Sewn by Susan Harmon and Dottie Lankard
Quilted by Joan Gamble

Chapter 4

Projects

The five projects here explore a variety of spiral types and techniques: *Spiraling Roses On My Table* is a table runner that uses three rose-shaped Nesting spirals. *Exploding Spiral* is a single, eight-sided Point-to-Point spiral embellished with appliqué. *The Court Jester* also uses an eight-sided, Point-to-Point spiral, adjusted to combine with nine-patch blocks. *Zowie! Powie!* (shown left) has eight-sided Point-to-Point spirals that change direction in each ring to create lightning bolts. *Synergy* uses creative coloring of a Baravelle spiral to create interwoven spokes.

As size goes, each project is fairly small so as not to be overwhelming. You can make them as shown, or increase the number of blocks to suit your needs.

Templates for all the projects can be found on the accompanying CD. You will need Adobe Reader on your computer to access the files. Most computers have it installed when they come from the manufacturer. If yours does not, it is available for free on the Internet.

The CD also contains a variety of templates for other spirals. You can use these as building blocks for a spiral quilt design, or take them as inspiration for creating your own unique spirals.

Spiraling Roses On My Table

PROJECT 1

*T*hese roses are made with five-sided Nesting spirals set in square blocks. Depending on how many blocks you create, you can make a pillow, table runner or quilt. Yardage given is for three blocks as shown here. This is a great project for using up scraps.

Supplies and tools

- White paper: 2 sheets 8½" × 11"
- Translucent foundation material: 3 sheets 8½" × 11"
- Thread for assembly: neutral or background color
- Thread for quilting
- Fabric glue stick
- See page 82–83 for foundation preparation tools
- See page 92 for sewing tools

Finished size: 18" × 42"
Skill level: Intermediate quilter, spiral beginner

Spiraling Roses on My Table
Designed by RaNae Merrill and Emma Krenek
Sewn and machine-quilted by Emma Krenek

Tips for Success

- The best fabrics for this project are tone-on-tones, textures and small prints in a single color.
- Choose any color for the rose, then use at least three different light fabrics, three medium ones and three dark ones in that color. Make sure all lights are lighter than mediums, and all mediums are lighter than darks.
- If you use a busy print in one spoke, place solid and/or strongly contrasting fabrics in the spokes on either side to "hold" the busy print.

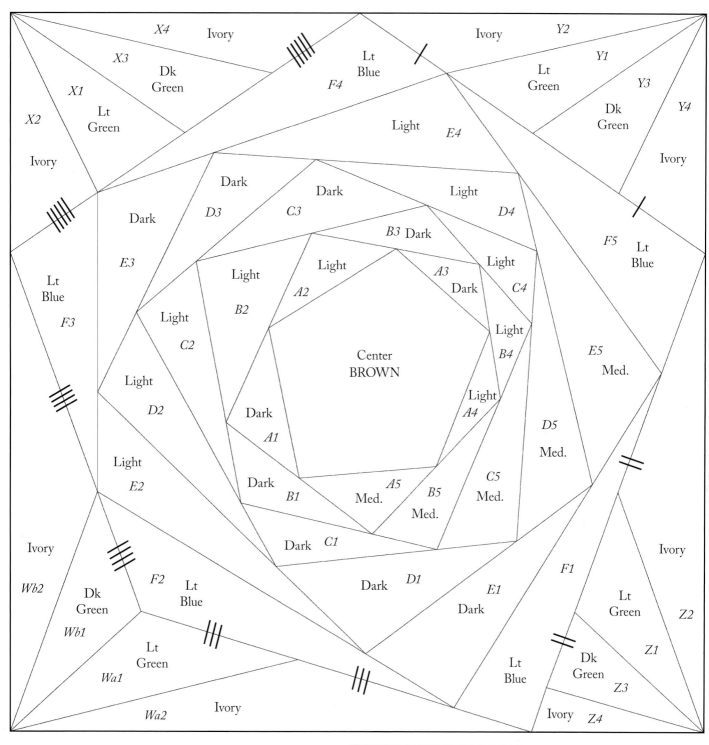

X4   Ivory   Lt Blue   Ivory   Y2

X3

X1   Dk Green   F4   Lt Green   Y1

X2   Lt Green   Light   E4   Y3

Ivory   Dk Green   Y4

Dark   Dark   Light   Ivory

Dark   D3   C3   D4

E3   B3 Dark   F5   Lt Blue

Light   Light   Light

Lt Blue   B2   A2   A3   C4

F3   Light   Dark   Light

C2   B4   E5

Light   Center   Light   Med.

D2   BROWN   A4

Light   Dark   D5   Med.

E2   A1

Dark   C5   Med.

Ivory   Dark   A5   B5

B1   Med.   Med.

Wb2   Dark   C1   Ivory

Dk Green   F2   Lt Blue   F1   Z2

Wb1   Dark   D1   E1   Lt Green

Lt Green   Dark   Z1

Wa1   Lt Blue   Dk Green   Z3

Wa2   Ivory   Ivory   Z4

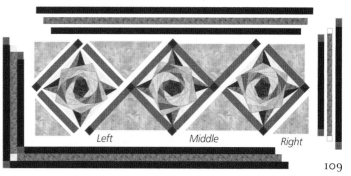

Left   *Middle*   *Right*

Assembly

Fabric Chart

All seams are ¼" unless indicated otherwise.
Measurements do not include extra yardage

Fabric	Yardage	Cut *(LOF = Length of fabric, WOF = Width of fabric)*
Light Blue: Background, outer ring of spiral	¾ yd	1 square 11⅞", then cut diagonally in both directions 2 squares 6¼", then cut diagonally in one direction 15 triangles from templates
Dark Blue: Inner and outer border, backing, binding	1⅜ yds	Cut on length of fabric: 2 strips 1½" × at least 41" 2 strips 1½" × at least 37" 2 strips 1½" × 16½" 2 strips 1½" × 12½" 1 backing 24" × LOF (includes 3" extra on each side for quilting frame) 3 strips 2½" × LOF (Join with 45-degree seams into a continuous strip.)
Light Green: Leaves, middle border	¼ yd	2 strips 1½" × WOF 2 strips 1½" × 14½" 12 triangles from templates
Dark Green: Leaves, sashing corner squares	¼ yd	10 squares 1½" 12 triangles from templates
Lights: Petals	⅛ yd total	30 triangles from templates
Mediums: Petals	⅛ yd total	15 triangles from templates
Darks: Petals	⅛ yd total	30 triangles from templates
Dark Pink: Sashing	¼ yd	12 strips 1½" × 8"
Ivory: Block background, border corner squares	¼ yd	24 triangles from templates 4 squares 1½"
Dark Brown: Center	less than ⅛ yd	3 from center template
Batting	26" × 50"	

1 Prepare the Foundations

On white paper make two copies of the template on page 109. (If the blocks will be different colors, make two copies for each different block.) On one copy, work out where your rose petal colors will go. Make sure there is contrast wherever triangles touch, particularly on the short sides. Write your final color choices on the other copy of the template; this will be your master. Make three copies of the master template on translucent foundation material.

2 Cutting

Cut fabric according to the cutting list above. Cut the large pieces of fabric first. Where measurements are given, cut pieces to that size. For spiral pieces, cut up the master templates along the lines. Use the Strip Method on page 89 for the rose petals; use the Template Method from page 88 for corner pieces.

3 Corners, Part 1

Cut off the leaf corners of the foundations. (See *Corners Diagram*, right.) Keep them with their corresponding blocks. Working in numerical order, piece each corner as a separate unit. Leave at least ¼" seam allowance on all edges. Use a light touch of fabric glue to hold the ivory pieces against the foundation. Do not remove foundation.

4 Sew Spirals

Sew spirals according to directions for sewing Nesting and Baravelle spirals on page 94. Leave at least ¼" seam allowance beyond the foundation edge on all sides. Do not remove the foundation.

5 Corners, Part 2

Reattach the corners to the spirals, matching edges of the foundation and alignment marks. Sew precisely at cut edges of the foundations.

6 Square Up

Square up the blocks, leaving ¼" seam allowance beyond the outer line of the foundation. Do not remove the foundation.

7 Arrange and Mark the Blocks

Arrange the rose blocks so each is rotated differently. Label the blocks Left, Middle and Right. Mark the top corner of each block. (See the *Assembly* illustration on page 109.)

8 Sashing

Sew sashing strips to the upper-right and lower-left side of each block. Sew green squares to both ends of two sashing strips. Sew two strips of Green square + sashing strip + Green square + sashing strip + Green square.

9 Join the Blocks

Following the *Assembly* illustration, sew either large or small light blue triangles to the upper right and lower left sides of rose blocks. Sew the longest sashing strips to the left and right sides of the Middle block/triangle group, matching all the seams. (Pin generously to prevent slipping, as you are sewing on the bias.) Sew sashing strips with green squares on both ends to the left side of the Left block/triangle group and the right side of the Right group. Join the Left and Right block/triangle) groups to the Middle group. Sew the light blue triangles to the upper-left and the lower right corners. Square up the edges, trimming ¼" outside of the corners of the green squares (see above right, *Trimming the Edges*).

10 Borders

Sew the small pink squares to both ends of each short inner and outer border strip. Sew small ivory squares to

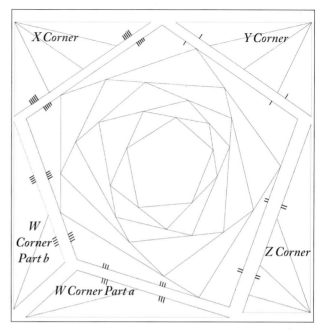

Corners Diagram
Piece each corner separately as shown, leaving ¼" seam allowance on all edges.

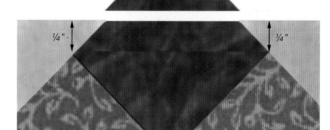

Trimming the Edges
When cutting off the corners of the foundations, leave at least ¼" seam allowance on all edges.

both ends of each short middle border strip. Sew long inner border strips to the long sides of the rose panel, then short inner border strips to the ends. Repeat for the middle border, then the outer border.

11 Quilting and Binding

If using removable foundation material, remove the foundation material now. Sandwich and baste the top, batting and backing. Quilt as desired. *Suggestion:* Simple stitch-in-the-ditch along the edges of the spokes and the edges of the triangles emphasizes the form of the petals and the spiral. After quilting, square up the edges. Follow instructions for binding on page 105.

Exploding Spiral

*T*his is a single eight-sided Point-to-Point spiral.

Supplies and tools

- White paper: 25 sheets 8½" × 11" and 1 square 40" × 40"

- Translucent foundation material: 1 sheet 8½" × 11". Can be paper, tear-away, leave-in or rinse-away.

- Translucent foundation material: 1 square at least 40" × 40": 1¼ yds if 44" wide, 2½ yds if 22" wide. Use a light-weight non-woven material such as Pellon. Can be leave-in, tear-away or rinse-away. Do *not* use paper.

- Thread for assembly: neutral or background color

- Shiny rayon thread in colors of dot fabrics for machine appliqué

- Heat-fusing material such as TransWeb or Steam-a-Seam: ⅝ yard (17" wide) or 10 sheets 8½" × 11"

- Medium-weight cardboard (cereal box weight): 8½" × 11" sheet

- Thread for quilting

- See page 82–86 for foundation preparation tools

- See page 90 for sewing and cutting tools

- Straightedge at least 24" long

Finished size: 41½" × 41½"
Skill level: Intermediate

Tips for Success

Because this spiral is large, it presents a good opportunity to use fabric with a large pattern. To maintain well-designed spokes, place a solid or pseudo-solid fabric between large-patterned spokes. Using a large pattern may eliminate the need for the applique dots. When using large prints, it may be necessary to funny-cut small pieces for color continuity in the spokes.

Exploding Spiral
Designed, sewn and hand-quilted by RaNae Merrill

Fabric Chart

All seams are ¼" unless indicated otherwise.
Measurements do not include extra yardage.

Fabric (Fabrics as shown)	Yardage	Cut (WOF = Width of fabric) Cut largest pieces first, smallest last
Color #1: Dark spokes (Black)	1⅜ yds	1 of each Color #1 spiral piece 4 of each Color #1 center piece
Color #2: Light spokes (White)	1 yd	1 of each Color #2 spiral piece 4 of each Color #2 center piece
Color #3: Dots and side border/bindings (Red)	½ yd	2 strips WOF × 4" *Dots:* Fuse fabric to fusible web. Cut at least 4 circles of each size. Cut more medium and small dots as needed.
Color #4: Dots and top border/binding (Blue)	⅜ yd	1 strip WOF × 4" *Dots:* Fuse fabric to fusible web. Cut at least 4 circles of each size. Cut more medium and small dots as needed.
Color #5: Dots and bottom border/binding (Yellow)	⅜ yd	1 strip WOF × 4" *Dots:* Fuse fabric to fusible web. Cut at least 4 circles of each size. Cut more medium and small dots as needed.
Backing and hanging sleeve		1¼ yds @ 44" wide (44" square, allows for 2" extension on each side) ¼ yd for hanging sleeve (optional)
Batting		44" square

1 Prepare the Foundations

Prepare one master template for the complete spiral according to directions on page 84–85. Mark colors on the master template. Trace all the lines and markings to the 40" square translucent foundation. Trace the center markings, including the gray dashed line 5" to the 6" × 6" square foundation material.

2 Cutting

Cut the fabric according to the cutting list above. Cut large pieces first. Where measurements are given, cut pieces to that size. For spiral pieces, cut up the master templates along the lines. Use the Template Method on page 88 to cut triangles and center pieces. For dots, cut templates from cardboard, then cut fused fabric to size; do not add seam allowance.

3 Assemble and Position the Center

Cut the center foundation in half along the dashed line through the center so pieces 1 through 4 are on one half and pieces 5 through 8 are on the other. Paper-piece each half in numerical order. Leave a ¼" seam allowance on the center cut edge. Join the halves and press. Trim the fabric and foundation along the dashed line surrounding the center. Set the center following the instructions on page 94.

Center Diagram

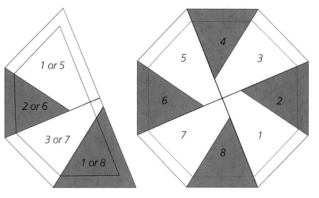

4 Sew the Spiral

Sew the spirals according to the Pinwheel and Point-to-Point directions on page 96. After the last ring of triangles, sew the four dark right-angle triangles to the dark spokes to fill out the square. Pin or baste all edges to the foundation. Square up the top, leaving ¼" seam allowance beyond the outer line on the foundation.

Overlap Diagram

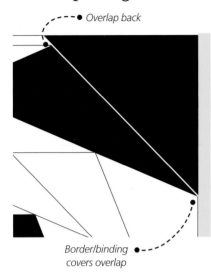

● *Overlap back*

Border/binding covers overlap ● - -

Adding the Border (Partial-Seam Piecing)

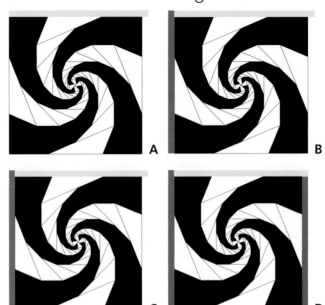

A B

C D

5 Border/Binding, Part 1

Look at the finished spiral. There will be a place at the edge of the corners where Color #1 fabric overlaps back from the line of the spoke. (See *Overlap Diagram* above.) This should fall right on the outer line of the foundation, and should be completely covered when you attach the border/binding.

On each strip of binding fabric, zigzag over the edge that will not be sewn to the quilt top, then press under ¼" on the same side. (You'll handle the quilt a lot before finishing, and you don't want the edges to fray.)

6 Border/Binding, Part 2

Now, you'll use partial-seam piecing (see *Adding the Border* diagram above) to attach the border. Place the starting edge of the top border strip even with the left raw edge of the quilt top. The strip should extend at least 2½" beyond the end of the side of the top. Sew the strip along the top edge, ending 2" from the right side of the quilt top (figure A). Flip open and press before sewing the next strip. Working counterclockwise, sew the next three strips to the edges of the top (figures B, C, D). Press open each strip before sewing the next one over it. Return to the end of the first strip that was left unstitched and complete the seam.

7 Dots

Arrange the dots on the light-colored areas of the spiral beginning with the smallest dots near the center and graduating to larger dots as you move out. Allow a few to overlap

into dark areas and over the borders. Fuse into place (follow manufacturer's instructions), then machine satin-stitch around the edges.

8 Quilting, Part 1

Sandwich and baste top, batting and backing. When you finish the binding, this extra batting will fill out the binding. Stitch-in-the-ditch at the edges of the spokes, but go around dots that cross edges of spokes. Quilt around each dot. Then, add more quilting, if desired. Stitch-in-the-ditch along the edges of the border/binding, but do not quilt over the border. Skip places where dots overlap the stitching line. For dots that overlap border/binding, wait until you have finished the binding (next step) and then quilt around them.

9 Border/Binding, Part 3

Trim *only the batting and backing* to 2" outside the stitching line of the border/binding, being careful not to cut the border/binding itself. Turn the pressed edge of the border/binding to the back side of the quilt. Blind-stitch by hand or stitch-in-the-ditch by machine over the border/binding seam line. At corners, turn under the end of the border/binding strips and hand-stitch into place.

10 Quilting, Part 2

After finishing the border/binding, quilt around any dots that overlap the border.

Tannenbaum Twist

*B*eth Bigler put an eight-sided Point-to-Point spiral to very practical and beautiful use in this festive Christmas tree skirt.

Tannenbaum Twist
40" × 40"
Designed, pieced and quilted by Beth Bigler

Adapting the Pattern

- Choose bright holiday fabrics.

- Leave out the center, corners, dots and borders.

- For artificial trees, no other adjustment is necessary. Put the tree skirt over the tree stand, then insert the trunk of the tree through the tree skirt into the base.

- A natural tree may need a larger hole in the middle to accommodate the trunk, so leave out one or two rings of triangles at the center of the spiral. Add a split in the spiral to allow the skirt to be wrapped around the base of the tree and to be opened when you water it. To make a split: Before piecing the spiral, cut the foundation along the edge of one spoke. Begin and end piecing each ring of triangles at this edge. Or, piece the spiral whole as in the instructions, then simply cut a straight line from the center to the edge.

- Use the binding method on page 105 to finish all raw edges.

The Court Jester

Supplies and tools

- White paper: 4 sheets 8½" × 11" or 1 square 13" × 13"

- Translucent foundation material: 16 sheets 8½" × 11" or 4 squares 13" × 13"
  Can be paper, non-woven tear-away, non-woven leave-in or rinse-away.

- Thread for assembly: neutral or background color

- Thread for quilting

- See page 86 for foundation preparation tools

- See page 90 for sewing tools

Finished size: 41" × 41"
Skill level: Intermediate

I have a stack of nine-patch blocks I inherited from my maternal grandmother, and each time I make a quilt for family I incorporate at least one of these vintage blocks. The challenge here was how to combine a very curvy spiral block with a very square nine-patch block.

The Court Jester
41" × 41"
Designed and sewn by RaNae Merrill
Machine-quilted by Gwen Baggett

Tips for Success

- Because the spirals have to align with the sides of a nine-patch block, the octagons are not the same length on all sides. Pay close attention to color and placement markings on the master template when cutting fabric and sewing.

- Since two spirals spin in the opposite direction from the two others, the Strip Method (page 89) is the best way to cut the fabric for the spirals. This method eliminates the possibility of cutting triangles in the wrong direction.

- Value contrast is very important to making this design appear. When choosing your fabrics, select a full range of values—dark, medium and light. Match the placement of the values to the positions in the photo above.

Fabric Chart

All seams are ¼" unless indicated otherwise.
Measurements do not include extra yardage.

Fabric *(Fabrics as shown)*	Yardage	Cut *(WOF = Width of fabric)*
Color #1: Spiral blocks, 9-patches blocks and diamond border (Yellow)	⅝ yd	*Diamond border:* • 1 strip WOF × 1½" • 4 squares 2" *Side 9-patch blocks:* 4 squares 1⅞" *Spiral blocks:* 4 each spiral template.
Color #2: Spiral blocks and diamond border (Coral)	⅜ yd	*Diamond border:* 1 strip WOF × 1½" *Spiral blocks:* 4 each spiral template
Color #3: (Spiral blocks and 9-patch blocks (Light pink)	1⅛ yds	*Side and corner 9-patch blocks:* • 5 squares 6⅞", then cut diagonally in both directions for 20 quarter-square triangles • 2 squares 3¾" then cut diagonally in one direction for 4 half-square triangles *Spiral blocks:* 4 each spiral template
Color #4: spiral blocks, 9-patch blocks, inner and outer border, diamond border (Black)	1¼ yd	*Inner border:* 4 strips WOF × 1½" *Diamond border:* 1 strip WOF × 1½" *Outer border:* 4 strips WOF × 1½" *Binding:* 4½ strips WOF × 2½" *Side 9-patch blocks:* • 8 rectangles 1⅞" × 3³⁄₁₆" • 4 squares 1⅞" *Spiral blocks:* 4 each spiral template
Color #5: 9-patch blocks, inner and outer border, diamond border (Magenta)	⅝ yd	*Diamond border:* 1 strip WOF × 1½" *Center & corner 9-patch blocks:* 8 squares 4½" *Side 9-patch blocks:* 4 squares 1⅞" *Inner & outer borders:* 8 squares 1½"
Color #6: 9-patch blocks (Photo shows two different fabrics because center 9-patch is vintage)	⅜ yd	*Center & side 9-patch blocks:* 13 squares 4½"
Color #7: 9-patch blocks, diamond border (White)	½ yd	*Diamond border:* • 8 strips WOF × 1½", then cut 3½" piece off end of each strip *Side 9-patch blocks:* 8 squares 1⅞"
Backing		2¾ yds: Cut 2 lengths of 49½"; sew together along selvages; trim to 49" square (allows for 4" extension on each side). 41" × 10" strip from leftover for hanging sleeve, if desired.
Batting		42" square (minimum)

Joining Blocks

Side Block

1 *Prepare the Foundations*

Prepare one master template for the spiral according to the directions on page 84. Print one master template on plain white paper and four foundations on translucent paper. Trace all the lines and markings to four translucent foundations. Mark the front of two translucent foundations as "Front," then turn over the other two foundations and mark the back as "Front." This will give you two pairs of opposite-spinning spirals.

2 *Cutting*

Cut according to the cutting list. Where measurements are given, cut pieces to that size. Cut large pieces first. For spirals, cut up the master template along the lines and use the Strip Method on page 88 (See note in *Tips for Success*). For each template piece, cut four rectangles at least ¾" wider and ¾" higher than the template. Keep the templates attached to the fabric.

3 *Sew Spirals*

Sew the spirals according to the Pinwheel and Point-to-Point directions on page 96. Sew two spirals of the same

direction at the same time to avoid confusion. Add the corners. Pin or baste all the edges to the foundation. Square up the blocks, leaving a ¼" seam allowance beyond outer line on foundations. Do not remove the foundation.

4 *Side Blocks*

Sew the side blocks according to the *Side Block* illustration above. After piecing the small 9-patch sections, square up this section of the block to 4½" if necessary, before joining to the other pieces.

5 *Join the Blocks*

Join the blocks in diagonal rows. Join the rows. (See *Joining Blocks* above left.) Use the outside lines of spiral foundations as seam lines. Square up the quilt top.

6 *Inner Border*

Sew a 1½" square to one end of each inner border strip. For the first border strip, align the seam line of the square on the end of the strip to the seam line on the foundation at the edge of the center panel (See figure A from *Adding Inner Border* on page 119). Beginning 1" from the square, sew

Adding the Inner Border

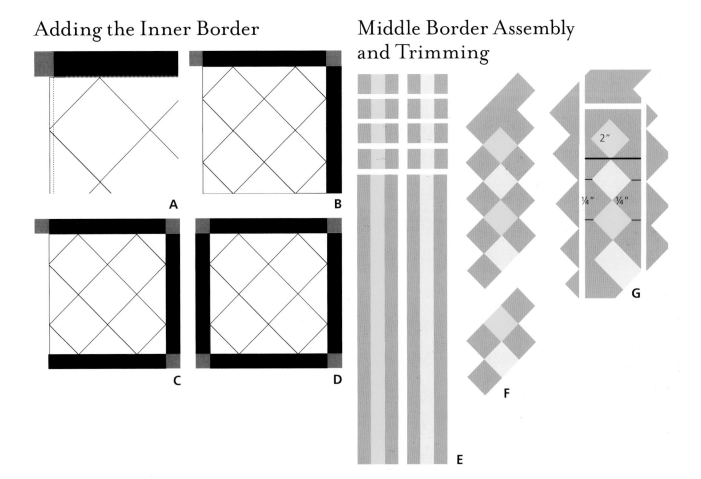

A

B

C

D

Middle Border Assembly and Trimming

E

F

2"

¼" ¼"

G

the border to the side of the center panel. Second through Fourth border strips (figures B, C, D): Working one at a time around the center panel, align the seam lines of the corner blocks to the seam lines of the previous border strip. After the fourth side, return to the first border strip and sew the loose end over the end of the fourth border strip. Trim the ends of the strips even with the sides.

7 *Middle Border (Diamonds)*

See *Middle Border Assembly and Trimming*, above right. Sew three 1½" strips together lengthwise as shown (figure E). Sew together strips Color #7-#1-#7 (White-Yellow-White), #7-#2-#7 (White-Coral-White), #7-#4-#7 (White-Black-White), #7-#5-#7 (White-Magenta-White). Press the seams toward the center strip.

Cut 3"-wide strips crosswise into 1½" units: 24 Color #1 (Yellow), 20 Color #2 (Coral), 20 Color #4 (Blue), 28 Color #5 (Magenta) (92 total).

Join 1½" strips diagonally as shown (figure F). Sew sixteen 4-unit strips #4-#2-#1-#5 (Black-Coral-Yellow-Magenta). Sew four 3-unit strips #4-#1-#5 (Black-Yellow-Magenta). Sew four 3-unit strips #4-#1-#2

(Black-Yellow-Coral). Join four strips of twenty-three units each: four 4-unit strips (all in the same direction), then sew one #4 (Black) unit to the end that is not #4 (Black). Sew a different 3-unit strip to each end, with a #4 unit (Black) at the ends. Sew a 1½" × 3" Color #7 (White) strip to each end.

Press the border strip well. Lay the strip on the cutting mat (do not stretch). Align the corners of the diamonds along the edge of a clear rotary cutting ruler so they are precisely straight. Using a rotary cutter, trim the strips to 2" wide, leaving ¼" seam allowance from the corner of the diamonds on each side and ends (figure G).

Sew a diamond border to the left and right sides of the quilt top. Sew a 2" end square to both ends of the two remaining diamond strips. Sew these strips to the top and bottom of the quilt top. Ease or stretch the strips slightly to fit, if necessary.

8 *Finish Quilt*

Use the same method as for the inner border. If using removable foundation, remove now. Sandwich and baste the top, batting and backing. Quilt as desired. Follow instructions for binding on page 105.

Zowie! Powie!

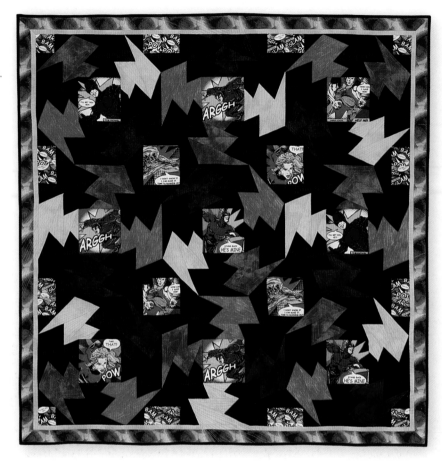

Supplies and tools

- White paper: 8 sheets 8½" × 11" or 2 squares 16" × 16"
- Translucent foundation material: 36 sheets 8½" × 11" or 9 squares 16" × 16" Can be paper, non-woven tear-away, non-woven leave-in or rinse-away.
- Thread for assembly— neutral or background color
- Thread for quilting
- See page 86 for foundation preparation tools
- See page 92 for sewing tools
- Removable marking pencil
- Fabric glue stick

Finished size: 55" × 55"
Skill level: Advanced

*T*he eight-sided Point-to-Point spirals change direction in each ring, resulting in a zigzag lightning bolt design.

Zowie! Powie!
49½" × 49½"
Designed by RaNae Merrill
Sewn by Susan Harmon and Dottie Lankard
Quilted by Joan Gamble

Tips for Success

The four interior corners (10, 11, 12 and 13 in the *Assembly* instructions, page 125) occur where corners of four spiral blocks meet. These corners are filled with a single piece of fussy-cut fabric. The individual blocks are first pieced, leaving an empty space in these corners. When blocks are joined, a window forms. The interior corner piece is then appliquéd from behind to fill the window with a single piece of fabric. If you don't want to use a single piece of fabric in these positions, simply piece in the entire corner in step 5 (you'll need 16 more squares 2¾" × 2¾" of Color #5).

Fabric Chart

All seams are ¼" unless indicated otherwise.
Measurements do not include extra yardage.

Fabric *(as shown)*	Yardage	Cut *(WOF = Width of fabric)*
Color #1: Zigzags in spirals (Red: Timeless Treasures Pat-1006 Poppy)	⅜ yd	9 of each Color #1 spiral piece
Color #2: Zigzags in spirals (Green: Timeless Treasures Pat-1006 Green)	⅜ yd	9 of each Color #2 spiral piece
Color #3: Zigzags in spirals, inner border (Yellow: Timeless Treasures Pat-1006 Lemon)	⅝ yd	9 of each Color #3 spiral piece. 5 strips 1" × WOF. Cut 1 strip into 4 equal pieces (10"+). Sew one 10" piece to each end of each remaining WOF strip to make 4 strips 1" × 50". Trim to correct length after attaching border.
Color #4: Zigzags in spirals (Blue: Timeless Treasures Pat-1006 Lapis)	⅜ yd	9 of each Color #4 spiral piece
Color #5: Squares along outer edge of center panel (Timeless Treasures GM-C9921)	¼ yd	20 squares 2¾" × 2¾" (See note about interior windows in *Tips for Success*, page 122. If you don't use a single piece of fabric, cut 16 more squares, total 36.)
Color #6: Outer border (Timeless Treasures GM-C9922)	½ yd	5 strips 2" × WOF. Cut 1 strip into 4 equal pieces (10" +). Sew one 10" piece to the end of each remaining WOF strip to make 4 strips 2" × 50". Trim to correct length after attaching border.
Color #7: Pictures for center squares and interior corner windows (Timeless Treasures GM-C9920)	½ yd, or enough to fussy-cut 13 squares	Fussy-cut 13 squares 5½" × 5½"; 9 for centers of spirals and 4 for interior corner windows (See note about interior windows. If you don't use a single piece of fabric in these, do not cut these 4 squares.)
Color #8: Background and binding (Black)	1⅞ yds	5 strips 2½" × WOF (210" total) for binding. Join with 45-degree seams into a continuous strip. 9 of each Background spiral piece 36 squares 3" × 3", then cut in half diagonally for corner units
Backing		3 yds: Cut to 2 lengths of 54"; sew together along selvages; Trim to 54" square (allows for 4" extension on each side). 49" x 10" strip from leftover for hanging sleeve, if desired.
Batting		50" square (minimum)

Master Templates

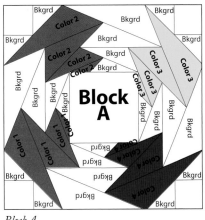

Block A

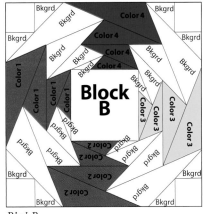

Block B

Piecing Za and Zb (Steps 3 and 4)

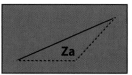
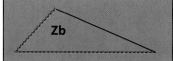

1. Mark the seam lines.

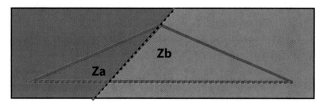

2. Join.

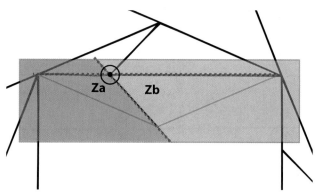

3. Sew onto the foundation.

1 *Prepare the Foundations, Part 1*

Prepare two master templates on white paper, one for Block A and one for Block B, according to directions on page 84. (EQ users, print two master templates on plain white paper and nine foundations on translucent paper.) Mark the colors for spirals only (not centers or corners) on the master template. Trace all the lines and markings onto nine translucent foundations. Make 5 of Block A and 4 of Block B.

2 *Prepare the Foundations, Part 2*

Following the color picture of the completed quilt and *Assembly* (page 126), place each translucent foundation in the position it will have in the quilt and number it, putting the number in the center and in the square in each corner. Mark the top of each block as it is positioned in the quilt. If the center pieces have an up/down orientation, mark the position of the top of each center piece. If the fussy-cut pieces for the centers and corner windows are different, mark which fussy-cut center goes in which block and in which corner window. Blocks 1, 2, 3, 4, 6, 7, 8 and 9 (all except 5) have some solid (S) and some window (W) corners: Mark which corners are solid and which are windows. (EQ users, mark registration lines at the corners.)

3 *Cutting*

Cut fabric according to the cutting list on page 121. Where measurements are given, cut pieces to that size. Cut the large pieces first. For spiral pieces, cut up the master templates along the lines. Use the Strip Method on page 89 to cut rectangular strips for triangles. Keep templates attached to the fabric.

With the removable marking pencil, mark the seam lines on the backs of pieces Za and Zb where they join and along the base (see *Piecing Za and Zb*, above).

4 *Sew the Spirals*

(Use directions for sewing Pinwheel and Point-to-Point spirals on page 96. Each ring of triangles changes direction, but this does not change the construction method.)

Position the center pieces in the correct position on each foundation.

Referring again to *Piecing Za and Zb*, join pieces Za and Zb into a single unit. Sew Za/Zb units onto the foundation, aligning the base line and the point where the Za/Zb seam line meets it with the base line and point lines on the foundation.

Sew each ring of triangles. Before adding the last ring of triangles, cut off the corners of the foundation. (This is why you marked the block number in each corner square. Keep the corners for each block with their corresponding block.) Sew on the last ring of triangles.

5 *Sew the Corner Units*

Refer to the *Piecing Corners* diagram on page 123. For solid corners (S), position a Color #5 square in the center square first. For window corners (W), leave this space empty. Place a triangle on one side. Sew along the seam line. Flip the triangle face up into position along the seam line. There should be at least ¼" seam allowance beyond the edges of the foundation. Use a light touch of fabric glue to hold the triangle against the foundation. Repeat for the second triangle. Reattach the corners to their corresponding spirals, matching block numbers and registration marks. Sew precisely along the edges of the foundation without catching them.

6 *Join the Blocks*

Join blocks 1-2-3, 4-5-6 and 7-8-9 into rows. Use the outside lines of the foundation as seam lines. Where there are windows, remove the empty square of foundation. Open up the folded edges of the triangles to join blocks, then

Assembly

Use this line drawing for positioning and marking individual blocks in the quilt. The asterisk (*) on each block indicates which spoke is Color #1 (red). You can also use this diagram to experiment with your own colors (enlarge as needed).

Piecing Corners

1. Place one triangle face down on front of the foundation. Stitch along the seam line.

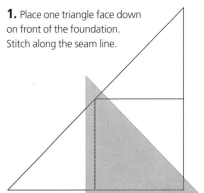

2. Flip fabric face up along seam line and press. Hold fabric in place with fabric glue.

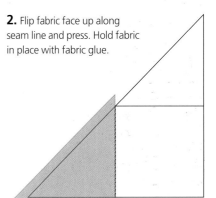

3. Place and stitch the triangle for the other corner the same way.

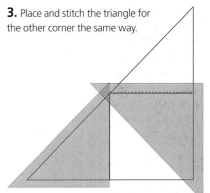

4. Flip and press.

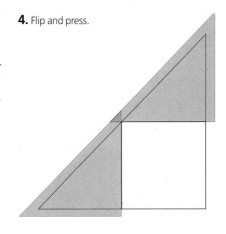

re-fold the edges of the joined triangles as a single edge, aligning with the edge of the foundation. Join the rows in the same manner.

7 Interior Corners

If using removable foundation, remove it from around the window opening. Place fussy-cut squares behind the windows at the interior corners (W). Pin, baste or glue into place. Using a thread that matches the background, sew the square into place with a narrow zigzag machine-stitch, or blind-stitch by hand.

8 Borders

Square up the top, leaving ¼" seam allowance beyond the outer line on foundations. If using removable foundation, remove the remaining foundation. Sew 1" Color # 3 (yellow) strips to each side, then to the top and bottom. Trim ends to even up with the sides of the center panel. Sew 2" Color #6 strips to each side, then to the top and bottom. Trim ends to even up with the sides of the center panel.

9 Quilting and Binding

Sandwich and baste top, batting and backing. Quilt as desired. Follow the instructions for binding on page 105.

PROJECT 5

Synergy

*F*our connecting Baravelle spirals are interwoven with double-direction spokes.

Supplies and tools

- White paper: 6 sheets 8½" × 11" or 1 square 17" × 17" and 1 strip 2½" × 17"

- Translucent foundation material: 24 sheets 8½" × 11" or 4 squares 17" and 4 strips 2½" × 17". Can be paper, non-woven tear-away, non-woven leave-in or rinse-away.

- Thread for assembly: neutral or background color

- Thread for quilting

- Fabric glue stick

- See page 82 for foundation preparation tools

- See page 92 for sewing tools

Finished size: 43½" × 43½"
Skill level: Advanced

Synergy
43½" × 43½"
Designed by RaNae Merrill
Sewn by Rhonda Adams and Kathy Edwards
Quilted by Gwen Baggett

Tips for Success

Strong contrast between the colors of the spokes and the background are essential for making the design clear and strong. Use solid colors, tone-on-tone or tiny prints that read as solids.

Fabric Chart

All seams are ¼" unless indicated otherwise.
Measurements do not include extra yardage.

*WOF strips will be cut down to short strips for piecing triangles in a spiral.

Fabric (as shown)	Yardage (as shown)	Yardage (your own colors)	Cut (WOF = Width of fabric, LOF = Length of fabric)	
Color #1: Background, large border and Gingko branch appliqués	4½ yds *Dark Plum:* Lonni Rossi Gingko Fantasy, Andover Fabrics Pattern #2681 Border print along sides of fabric is not used.	2 yds A dark tonal or other fabric with strong contrast to all fabrics in spirals	For as-shown version: fussy-cut 6 appliqués from gingko motif, then cut remaining pieces. Piece border strips if necessary. 2 strips 45" × 4¼" / 2 strips 37" × 4¼" / 8 squares 6½", cut in half diagonally / 8 Sashing Piece A (add ¼" seam allowance)	5 strips WOF × 1¼"* / 5 strips WOF × 1⅜"* / 5 strips WOF × 1½"* / 1 strip WOF × 1⅝"* / 2 strips WOF × 1¾"* / 4 strips WOF × 2"*
Color #2: Inner border and spoke extending from border	⅔ yd *Gold:* Textile Creations Echo Lame Gold	⅔ yd A bright color that reads as a solid. Decide whether this or Color #3 will be the brightest of the three spiral colors.	4 strips WOF × 1½" for inner borders / 2 strips WOF × 1¼"* / 2 strips WOF × 1⅜"* / 2 strips WOF × 2"* / 1 strips WOF × 2½"*	
Color #3: Opposite direction spiral and sashing	⅔ yd *Lavender:* Island Batiks G16-NPU-N	⅔ yd A bright color that reads as a solid with strong contrast to Color #2	5 strips WOF × 1¼"* / 3 strips WOF × 1½"* / 3 strips WOF × 2"* / 2 strips WOF × 2½"* / 8 Sashing Piece B (Add ¼" seam allowance)	
Color #4: Background spokes and sashing	¾ yd *Black with gold metallic overprint:* Kaufman Imperial Collection D#5905	¾ yd A color that reads as a solid lighter than the background and darker than the other spokes.	3 strips WOF × 1⅛"* / 2 strips WOF × 1¼"* / 2 strips WOF × 1⅜"* / 2 strips WOF × 1½"*	2 strips WOF × 1¾"* / 2 strips WOF × 2"* / 2 strips WOF × 2½"* / 4 Sashing Piece C (Add ¼" seam allowance)
Color #5: Outer border/ binding	⅜ yd *Black with gold metallic lines:* Lonni Rossi Harvest Dance Geisha, Andover Fabrics Pattern #3267	⅜ yd A color that frames the entire design	*As shown:* 6 strips LOF × 2½" (Sew 2" × 3" strips together end-to-end) 4 strips WOF × 2½" (Sew 2" × 2" strips together end-to-end)	*Your own colors:* 4½ strips WOF × 2½" (Piece as necessary for 4 strips 2½" × 45")
Appliqué	Included in yardage for Color #1 as shown	As much as needed to fussy-cut side and center motifs. If desired, centers of spirals can also contain appliqué.	Fussy-cut as needed	
Backing and hanging sleeve	53 yds: Cut to 2 lengths of 54"; sew together along selvages; trim to 54" square. 42" × 10" strip from leftover for hanging sleeve, if desired.			
Batting	45" square (minimum)			

Assembly

Use this line drawing to experiment with your own color choices (enlarge as needed).

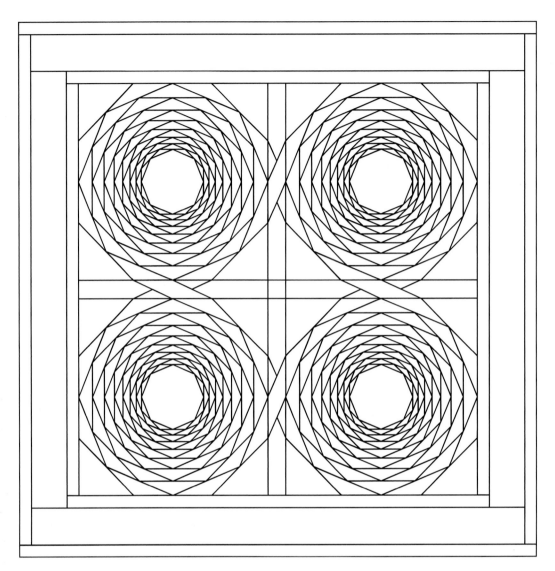

1 *Prepare Foundations*

Follow the directions on pages 83–86 for preparing foundations. Mark one master template for the spiral block and one for the sashing. Make four copies of each master template on translucent foundation material. Cut up the master template of sashing to use for cutting fabric.

2 *Cutting*

Cut fabric according to the cutting list. For sashing pieces, add ¼-inch seam allowance to templates. Pieces for the spirals are cut in width-of-fabric (WOF) strips. Cut the WOF strips as you work to the widths needed, beginning with the narrowest width first. As you sew the spiral, cut down the WOF strips to the lengths needed for triangles. (See *Strip Method* on page 89.) Sew these rectangular pieces into place on the spiral foundation, then trim to the triangle shape after sewing.

3 *Assemble the Spirals*

Follow the directions on page 94 for sewing Baravelle spirals. On very small triangles, trim seam allowances to ⅛". Pay close attention to the markings on the foundation for color placement. Do not remove foundation.

4 *Assemble the Sashing*

Cut the foundation on one of the diagonal lines and paper-piece each section. Use a touch of fabric glue to hold the A pieces together. Sew the two sections back together using the cut edges of the paper as a guide for the seam line. Do not remove the foundation.

5 *Assemble the Spirals and Sashing*

Sew one sashing strip to the side of each spiral block. Take care to match the edges of the sashing to the corresponding spokes of the block where marked on the foundation. Do not remove the foundation.

Variations

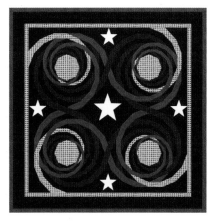

Floral Variation
Alternate version using a floral background and appliqués, with two shades of green for Color #4.

Regal Variation
Alternate version using fabrics from Kaufman's Imperial Collection for applique and borders.

Star Variation
Alternate version using star appliqué in the centers of the spirals.

6 *Join the Spirals*
Turn and arrange the blocks so the Color #2 spokes are oriented as in the picture of the quilt. Sew two pairs of blocks together, then join the two pairs. Be careful to match the edges of the sashing to the corresponding spokes of the block. There will be a hole in the center of the quilt that will be covered by the appliqué fabric. Do not remove the foundation.

7 *Appliqué*
Use your preferred method of appliqué (fusible, needle-turn, freezer paper, broderie perse, etc.) to appliqué the designs in the side spaces, the center and, if desired, the centers of the spirals.

8 *Borders*
If necessary, square up the center section of the quilt before adding borders. Sew two Color #2 border strips to the top and bottom. Trim ends even with the sides of the center panel. Sew two Color #2 border strips to the left and right sides. Trim ends even with the top and bottom of the center panel. Sew the 37" Color #1 border strips to top and bottom of the center panel. Trim ends even with the sides. Sew the 45" Color #1 border strips to the left and right sides. Trim ends even with the top and bottom. If using removable foundation, remove the foundation now.

9 *Quilting*
Quilt as desired. *Suggestion:* Outline the appliqué and spokes and avoid stitching over them. Use stippling or some other type of stitching in the background—especially between the spokes—that will flatten the background a bit and let the colored spokes raise up.

10 *Border and Binding*
If necessary, square up the quilt before adding binding. Press each binding strip in half lengthwise and press under ¼" seam allowance on one edge. Pin unpressed edges of two Color #5 strips ¾" from the raw edges of the left and right sides of the quilt. (If using Harvest Dance Geisha fabric, these should be the LOF strips.) Sew with ¼" seam. Trim ends even with top and bottom. Pin unpressed edges of two Color #5 border strips ¾" from the raw edges of the top and bottom. Sew with ¼" seam allowance. Trim the ends even with the left and right sides. ** Turn the left and right side strips to the back. Hand-stitch the pressed edge over the seam. Fold the top and bottom strips to the back, folding the ends slightly diagonally in from the corners. Hand-stitch the pressed edge over the seam.

11 *** Hanging Sleeve (optional)*
Add the hanging sleeve at ** in the binding instructions above, before finishing binding. Press a 42" × 10" strip of fabric in half lengthwise and finish ends with a ¼" rolled hem. On the back of the quilt, place the raw edges of the sleeve at the top edge of the quilt. The hemmed ends of the sleeve should fall just inside the sewing line of the side binding strips. Stitch along the top edge of the quilt just outside the binding seam. Trim seam allowance to ¼". Hand-stitch the bottom edge of the sleeve into place. Finish binding from ** in step 10 above.

Gallery of In-Spiralling Quilts

*N*ow that you're familiar with the different spirals, this *Gallery* will show you how a variety of quilters have used them in their quilts. Along with the photo of each quilt, I'll tell you what kind of spirals they used. Quilts with this symbol—  —are on the Spiromaniacs Blog at **http://spiromaniacs.wordpress.com**. You can follow that quiltmaker's process as she developed the design and completed the quilt. Just look for the quiltmaker's name under *Work In Progress Pages: Spiromaniacs II.*

    Almost every quilt in this book was made by someone who had never seen or made a spiral quilt before. I hope these will excite and inspire you as you think about making your first Simply Amazing Spiral Quilt—and many more after that!

Infinite Rainbow
60" × 60"
Designed, pieced, appliquéd and hand-quilted by RaNae Merrill

Double Rainbow

The sixteen-sided Point-to-Point spiral is a double rainbow. The satin star in the center is partly pieced and partly appliquéd. Shades of light and dark in both the rainbow and the star help create the illusion of depth and dimension.

Out of Africa
The designer used a twenty-one-sided Point-to-Point spiral in an irregular oval, with both smooth and feathered spokes.

Photo Op?!
38" × 54"
Designed and pieced by Jamie McClenaghan
Machine-quilted by Gwen Baggett

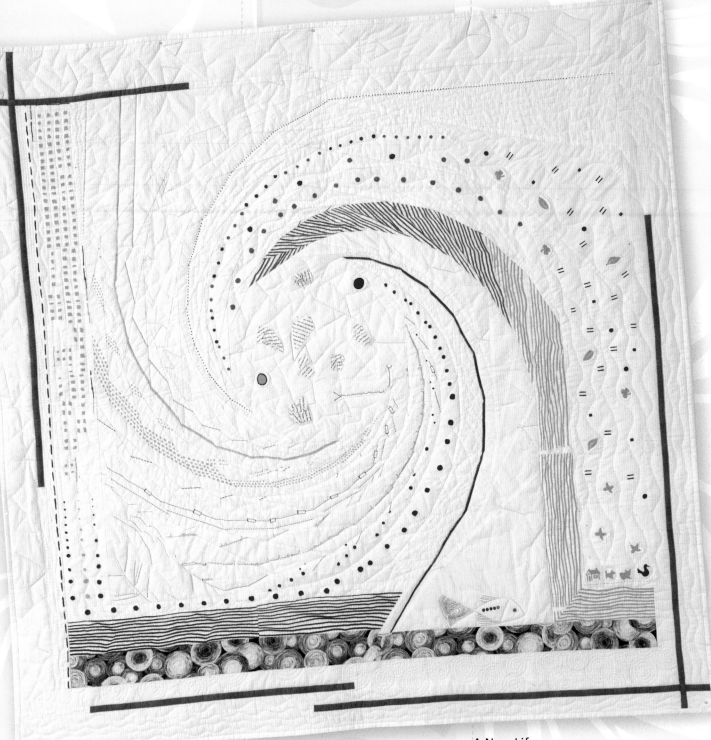

City Tears to Country Smiles
56" × 57"
Designed, pieced and hand-quilted by RaNae Merrill

A New Life
This is a circular twelve-sided Point-to-Point spiral, finished out to a square. Fabrics by Japanese designer Yoshiko Jinzenji were fussy-cut to form the continuous curved lines. This quilt tells the story of a transition in the life of a friend.

Spiral of Life
43½" × 43"
Designed, pieced and machine-quilted by Susanne Schmid

On the Contrary

A single Baravelle spiral gets dramatic treatment with a very contrary red spoke spinning in opposite direction to the other two and breaking the boundary of the border. By cutting a linear pattern perpendicular to the base of the triangles, Susanne was able to create a sense of explosion in the background.

Experimenting With Form

This quilt and table runner explore different ways to color eight-sided Baravelle spirals—spokes, double spokes, changing direction, rings and various non-spiral designs.

Enjoy the Journey,
36" × 36"
Designed and sewn by Micki Wiersma
Machine-quilted by Diane Anderson

Over the Rainbow
20" × 70"
Designed and sewn by Micki Wiersma
Machine-quilted by Diane Anderson

In Memory of Marja
44½" × 38¼"
Designed, pieced, appliquéd and
machine-quilted by Fee Bricknell

Small in Size, But Big Impact
Though the spirals (eight-sided Point-to-
Point spirals) are secondary to the central
flower, they add a strong dynamic element
to the overall design.

Short-Sided and Sassy
The designer worked with square Nesting spirals, set off-center in various ways by using different lengths on the short sides of the triangles.

Splish Splash Spirals
54" × 54"
Designed, sewn and machine-quilted by Muriel Roberts

Long-Sided and Luminous

Robin was inspired by Lucy Pringle's photos of crop circles (www.lucypringle.co.uk). By making the sides of the outer shapes longer on one side than on the other, she was able to throw the six-sided Baravelle spirals off-center.

Crop Circles: How'd They Do That?

72" × 95"
Designed, pieced, appliquéd and machine-quilted by Robin Armstead

Sails & Waves
84" × 104"
Designed and pieced by RaNae Merrill
Machine-quilted by Linda Taylor

Come Sail Away
Pinwheel spirals form the triangles in the center and corners; single spokes form the "waves."

A Cyclone of Color

Dottie used a ten-sided Point-to-Point spiral for the center, then added five-sided Nesting spirals (one spoke colored, four spokes black) to form the rays. Look closely to find the secondary spiral that forms the "yellow brick road."

We're Not In Kansas Anymore!

50" × 50"

Designed and sewn by Dottie Lankard
Machine-quilted by Cozetta Campbell

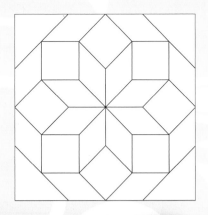

Fabulous Flames

The same irregular five-sided Nesting spiral set in a square block is the basis for all these spiral blocks. Electric Quilt software allowed Evelyn to easily set the square block in a diamond shape around the circle. This quilt and the one at right are examples of block-as-quilt settings, and both use the same layout. (See *Block-as-Quilt Setting*, page 61.)

Good Gracious Great Ball of Fire!
52" × 52"
Designed, sewn and machine–quilted by Evelyn Larrison

Shining Star

In this tribute to her mother, Barbara combined Baravelle spirals in the squares with mirrored pairs of Pinwheel spirals in the center star and outer diamonds. Moda Marble Ombre fabrics create the glowing gradations. This quilt has the same underlying layout as the one on the previous page.

Ellen's Star Rising
84" × 84"
Designed, sewn and machine–quilted by Barbara Baker

**Majestic Mandalai—
A Personal Journey**
47½" × 47½"
Designed and sewn by Rhonda Adams
Machine-quilted by Diane Anderson

Fans, Ribbons and Trunks
Rhonda began with a Dresden Plate layout. She cut across each of the twelve "wedges" to create a triangle and a pentagon and placed a Pinwheel spiral in each shape. By placing the same colors where spokes meet, she created yellow fans, purple and green ribbons, and orange trunks. (See *Mandalas*, page 63.)

Whirlygig
26" × 26"
*Designed, sewn and machine-
quilted by Julie Willis*

Feathered Spokes
Wedge-shaped Nesting spirals form the
center. The center is surrounded by a single
eight-sided spiral with feathered spokes. (See
Feathered Spokes, page 33.)

Carefully Colored

Bev and Barb explored ways that square spirals could be colored to create unique forms. They drank a lot of wine together in the process, hence the name and the appliqué grapes around the center!

Bev, Barb & a Bottle of Wine
84" × 84"

Designed, pieced, appliquéd and machine-quilted by Bev Anderson and Barb Porter

Fruit Salad Spinner
41" × 41"
Designed and pieced by RaNae Merrill
Machine-quilted by Gwen Baggett

Do You See?
32" × 43"
Designed and sewn by Kathy Oppelt
Quilted by Peggy Barkle

No Two Are Alike

Each of these snowflakes measures 6 to 7 inches in diameter. One has about 130 pieces; the other two each have over 250. Each is made of hexagons or pentagons around a central hexagon.

Resources

*M*any of the tools and materials used in this book are available from RaNae Merrill at www.ranaemerrillquilts.com, or your local quilt shop, or order from the manufacturer/publisher.

FOUNDATION MATERIALS

EQ Printables Foundation Sheets:
The Electric Quilt Company
(800) 356-4219
www.electricquilt.com

Simple Foundations Translucent Vellum Paper:
C&T Publishing, Inc.
(800) 284-1114
www.ctpub.com

Sulky products:
For information or to find a retailer:
(800) 874-4115
www.sulky.com

FABRIC SEARCH ENGINES

Quiltropolis:
www.webstore.quiltropolis.net

FabShopHop:
www.fabshophop.com/fabsearch.asp

GRADATED COLOR FABRICS

Hand-dyed sueded cottons:
Cherrywoods
(888) 298-0967
www.cherrywoodfabrics.com

Tone-on-tone fabrics in gradated palettes:
Jinny Beyer Studio
(866) 759-7373
www.jinnybeyer.com

Fabric medleys, gradated tonals and prints:
Keepsake Quilting Catalog
(800) 865-9458
www.keepsakequilting.com

Bali Blenders fabrics:
Available at local quilt shops

Moda Ombres fabrics:
Available at local quilt shops

TOOLS

Tools and materials used in this book are available from RaNae Merrill at www.ranaemerrillquilts.com

Add-a-Quarter and Add-an-Eighth tools are available at local quilt shops.

Seam rollers are available at www.justcurves.biz or at art supply stores. Get one with a barrel-shaped, not cylindrical, roller. They are also referred to as "brayers."

RECOMMENDED READING

The Experts' Guide to Foundation Piecing: 15 Techniques and Projects by Jane Hall (C&T Publishing, 2006)

Quilt Mavens: Perfect Paper Piecing by Deb Karasik and Janet Mednick (American Quilter's Society, 2007)

Visual Coloring: A Foolproof Approach to Color-Rich Quilts by Joen Wolfrom (C&T Publishing, 2007)

Color Play: Easy Steps to Imaginative Color in Quilts by Joen Wolfrom (C&T Publishing, 2000)

www.echalk.co.uk/amusements/opticalillusions/illusions.htm

The Artist's Way: A Spiritual Path to Higher Creativity by Julia Cameron (Jeremy P. Tarcher/Putnam, 2002)

Fabric-Finding Tips

- Fabric companies produce design- and color-coordinated fabric collections.
- Many companies now produce value-gradated and color-gradated fabrics.
- Some quilting catalogs package bundles of gradated fabrics.
- Packets of gradated hand-dyes are available from a number of companies or, if you like dyeing, dye your own.
- The Internet gives you access to thousands of fabrics. Be aware when shopping for fabric online that computer monitors often do not show color accurately.

Yardage Calculation Chart *See page 87 for detailed instructions on use of this chart.*

Fill out one chart (both pages) for each fabric in the quilt.

This worksheet is a tool, but since designs vary, it cannot be guaranteed to be 100 percent accurate in all cases. If in doubt, buy generously!

Fabric Description: _____

Name / Manufacturer / Inventory Number: _____

Where used in design: _____

Fabric Swatch Here

Part 2: Fabric for Spirals

	Height + ¾"	Length + ¾"	How Many Lg?	
Largest Spiral Triangle in Quilt	____	× ____	× ____ = ____ (A)	Square inches for each large triangle*
Smallest Spiral Triangle in Quilt	Height + ¾" ____	Length + ¾" × ____	How Many Sm? × ____ = ____ (B)	Square inches for each small triangle*

Multiply (A) × (B) Triangle in Quilt = ____ (C) — These numbers calculate a weighted average size for all triangles of this fabric in all spirals

How Many Lg + How Many Sm = ____ (D)

Divide (C) / (D) = ____ (E) — Average square inches for each triangle in spirals

Total Number of Triangles in All Spirals of this Fabric = ____ (F) — Count from template(s)

Special Yardage Needs:

Multiply (E) × (F) = ____ (G) — Total square inches of fabric for triangles in spirals

Divide by 1440 = ____ — Square inches in one yard of fabric (36" × 40" = 1,440 sq. in.)

Yardage of this fabric for triangles in spirals (Convert to yards. Round up to nearest 1/8 yard.) Add additional yardage for special needs, if necessary

Optional: Add'l yardage for special needs + ____ = ____ (H) — Yards

Total yards of this fabric for triangles in spirals, including special needs

Fussy-cutting, large prints and border prints: Buy the number of repeats of the pattern needed for your design.

Stripes: Depending on the direction you intend to cut, you may need up to three times the amount of fabric calculated here. To be sure, lay templates on fabric and physically measure the fabric needed.

Borders: If you prefer not to piece borders or large pieces longer than the width of the fabric, buy at least the length of the border strips and/or long pieces you want to cut.

Part 2: Fabric for Other Parts of Quilt (not spirals)

Description	Height + ¾"	×	Length + ¾"	×	How Many?	=	Column OPQ	Square inches**	Decimal to Yards Conversion	Swatch/Fabric Name
Spiral Centers		×		×		=				
		×		×		=			.125 = ⅛ yd	
		×		×		=			.25 = ¼ yd	
		×		×		=			.375 = ⅜ yd	
		×		×		=			.5 = ½ yd	
		×		×		=			.625 = ⅝ yd	
		×		×		=			.75 = ¾ yd	
		×		×		=			.875 = ⅞ yd	
		×		×		=				
		×		×		=				
Background		×		×		=				
Borders		×		×		=				
Backing		×		×		=				
Binding		×		×		=				

	Column OPQ		Notes
Total Column OPQ		= _____	Total square inches of this fabric for other parts of quilt
Divide by 1440		= _____	Square inch in one yard of fabric (36" × 40" = 1440 sq. in.)
		_____	Yardage of this fabric for triangles in other parts of quilt. (Convert to yards. Round up to nearest 1/8 yard.) Add additional yardage for special needs, if necessary
Add'l yardage for special needs		+ _____	yards
	(J)	= _____	Total yards of this fabric for triangles in other parts of quilt, including special needs
Add (H) + (J)		= _____	GRAND TOTAL of this fabric for all pieces in quilt

** The calculations in Part 1 assume that triangles will be cut as rectangles, then trimmed after sewing (Strip Method). For Template Method, yardage requirements may be as much as 25 percent less.

The calculations in Part 2 assume that irregular shapes will be cut as rectangles, then trimmed after sewing (Strip Method). For right-angle triangles and equilateral triangles, the number of square inches may be divided in half if desired.

All measurements assume ⅜" seam allowance in order to build in a bit of extra yardage. When sewing, use ¼" seam allowance unless otherwise indicated.

Template Library

*O*n the following pages are some basic templates you can photocopy for experimenting and coloring, or to use as building blocks for a quilt of your own. You will also find these and more templates on the CD that accompanies this book, in PDF and Electric Quilt versions.

Each template here gives a measurement that you can use as a basis for enlarging it. Use the table below to figure out how much to enlarge it for your needs. If you want a mirror image of the template, either photocopy it in mirror image mode, or photocopy it onto translucent vellum and turn it over. If you want to enlarge bigger than the size of a single sheet of paper, divide the template into several sections with pencil lines. Copy each section then use the lines as guides to assemble the spiral.

100%	1"	2"	3"
125%	1¼"	2½"	5"
150%	1½"	3"	6"
200%	2"	4"	8"
250%	2½"	5"	10"
300%	3"	6"	12"
400%	4"	8"	16"

Triangle Spirals

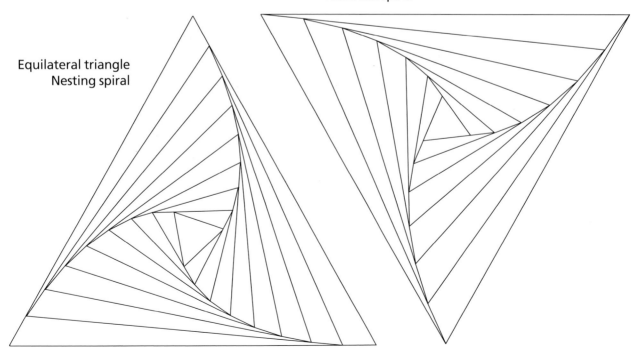

Equilateral triangle
Pinwheel spiral

Equilateral triangle
Nesting spiral

Right angle triangle Pinwheel spiral,
half-width increment on long side

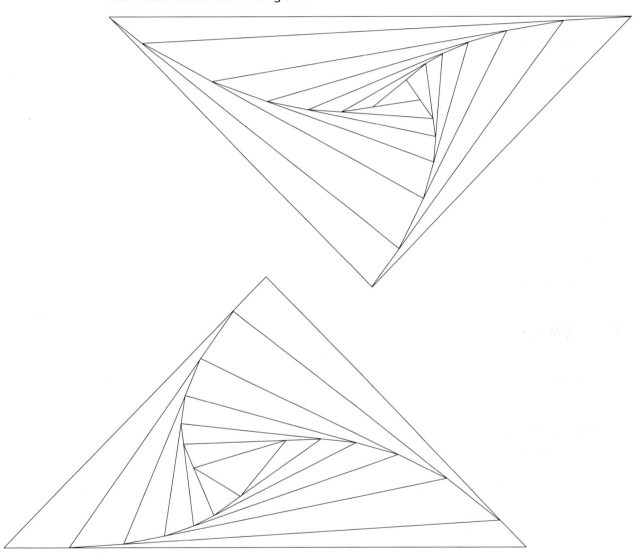

Right angle triangle Nesting spiral, half-width
increment on long side

Square Spirals

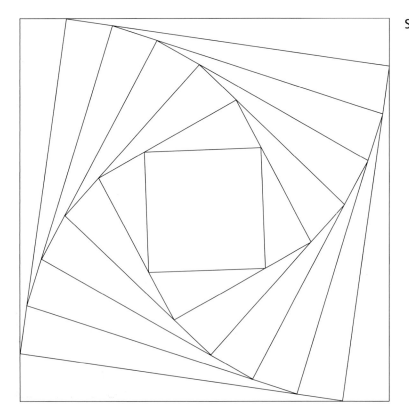

Square Nesting spiral

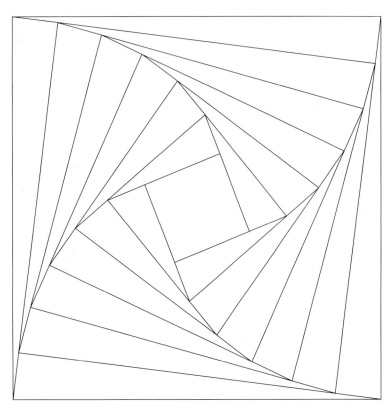

Square Pinwheel spiral

More Square Spirals

Off-center 1 square
Nesting spiral

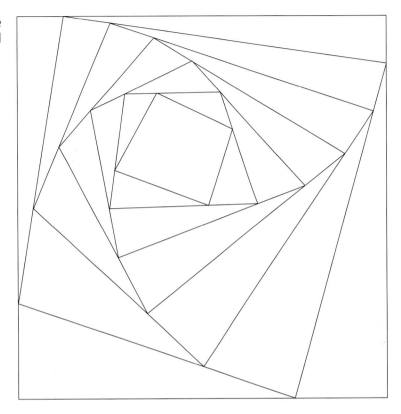

Off-center 2 square
Nesting spiral

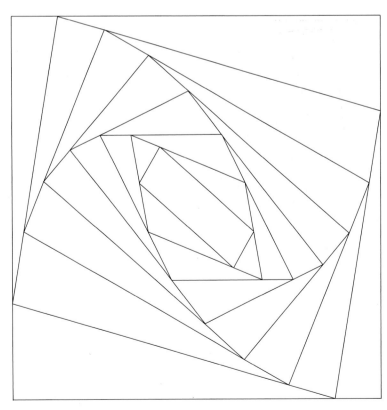

Five- and Six-sided Spirals

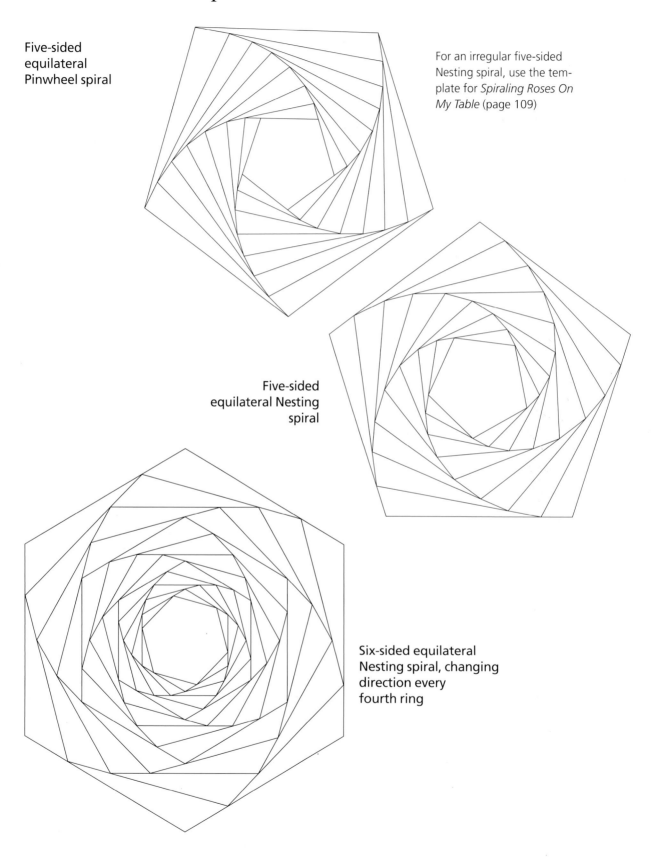

Five-sided
equilateral
Pinwheel spiral

For an irregular five-sided
Nesting spiral, use the tem-
plate for *Spiraling Roses On
My Table* (page 109)

Five-sided
equilateral Nesting
spiral

Six-sided equilateral
Nesting spiral, changing
direction every
fourth ring

Six-sided Spirals

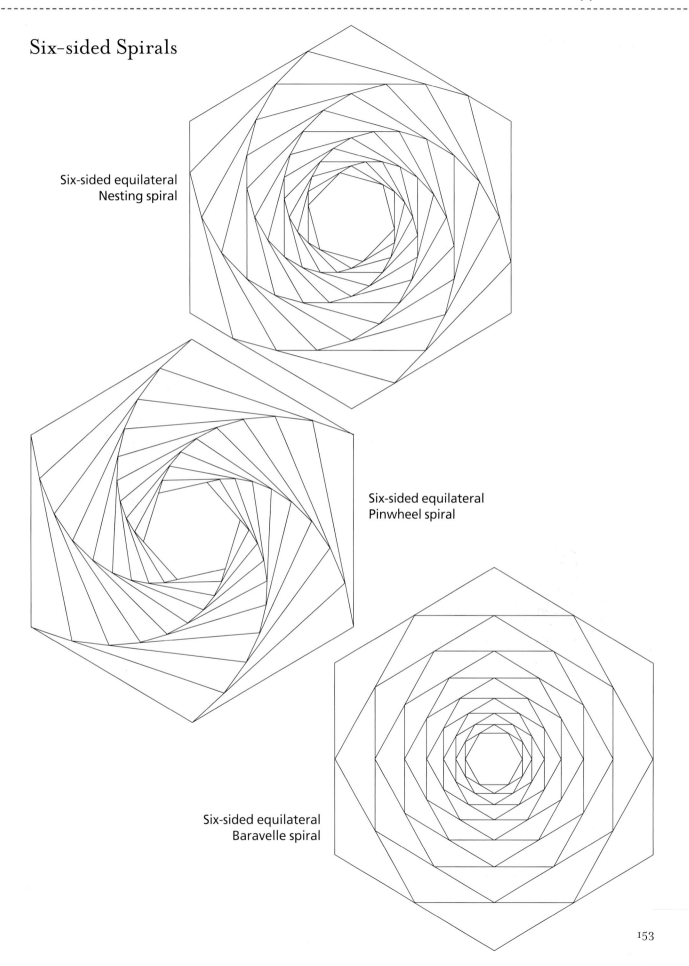

Six-sided equilateral
Nesting spiral

Six-sided equilateral
Pinwheel spiral

Six-sided equilateral
Baravelle spiral

Eight-sided Spirals

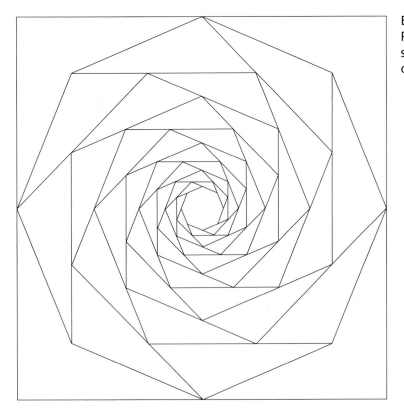

Eight-sided equilateral
Point-to-Point
spiral, points to sides
of square block

Eight-sided equilateral
Point-to-Point spiral, sides
to sides of square block

More Eight-sided Spirals

Eight-sided equilateral Nesting spiral,
sides to sides of square block

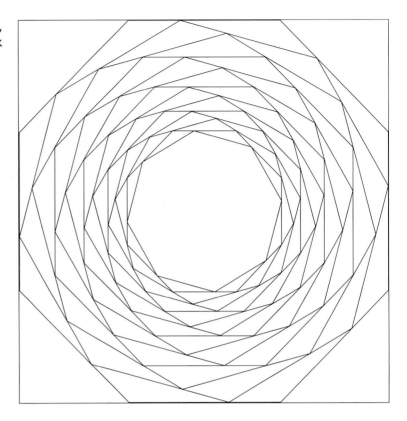

Eight-sided equilateral
Baravelle spiral,
sides to sides of square
block, with sashing

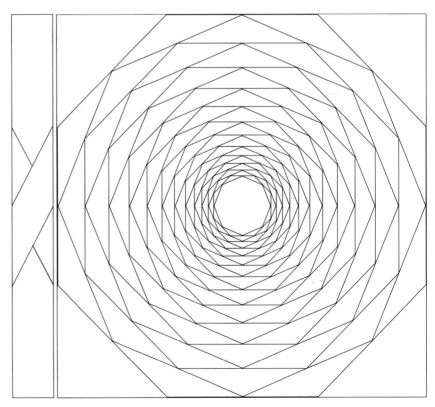

Twelve-sided Spirals

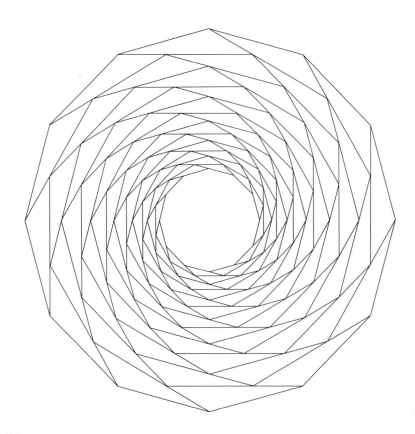

Twelve-sided Point-to-Point spiral

A

Alternating increments, 43
Appliqués, 56, 58, 66

B

Backgrounds, 55
Bar joins, 51
Baravelle, James, 16
Baravelle spirals, 9, 16–19, 31,
    124-127
  connecting, 48–49
  drawing, 16–19
  sewing, 94–95
Bev, Barb & A Bottle of Wine,
    15, 32, 45, 142
Big Bang + One Second, 16, 77
Binding, 105
Black and white, values in, 69
Blending, of fabric and color,
    68, 71–72, 79
Block-as-Quilt setting, 61–62,
    138-139
Blocks, joining, 103
Blue Sphere Experiment, 34
Books, on creativity and
    quilting, 145
Borders, 66–67, 78, 87
Bow Tie block, 61
Breaking the rules, 38–39
Brightly Churned, 51
Broderie perse flowers, 56

C

Centers, 11, 50, 52–54
Changes, to sewn pieces, 104
Christmas tree skirt, 117
City Tears to Country Smiles, 130
Color charts, 79
Color schemes, 68
Color theory, 68
Colors
  blending, 68, 71–72
  complementary, 73, 79
  contrasting, 44, 59
  dominant and secondary,
      70, 72–73
  gradation of, 76
  inversion, 73, 76

kicker, 68
  placement of, 71
  selection of, 68–70
  solid, 70
  of thread, 104
Connections, 45–51, 105–106
  problems and solutions, 47–51
Contrast
  and separation, 73
  in values, 69
Corners, 53–54, 111
Court Jester, The, 116–119
Creation, 12
*Crop Circles: How'd They Do
    That?*, 19, 43, 137

D

Dark Star/Spiral of Life, 60
Diamond-in-the-Square block, 62
Directional changes, 40–41
Do You See?, 37, 46, 144
Dominant colors, 70, 72–73
Double rainbow, 128
Double spokes, 32, 124
Double-width centers, 50
Drawing process, 9, 12–27, 83
Dresden Plate layout, 140
Drunkard's Path block, 57

E

Edges, 22, 44, 99-102
Eight-sided spiral templates,
    154–155
Electric Quilt, 61, 148
Ellen's Star Rising, 139
Enjoy the Journey, 32, 35, 37, 132
EQ Printables Foundation
    Sheets, 86
Equilateral shapes, 10
Era, and fabrics, 74
Eraser, 82
Exploding Spiral, 27, 112–114

F

Fabric, 88, 146. *See also*
    Muslin; Organza; Pellon;
    Yardage, calculating
  blending, 68, 71–72

  border print, 78, 82, 146
  cutting, 88–89, 102
  directional print, 78, 87
  finding, 148
  fussy-cut, 87, 122, 132, 146
  geometric print, 82
  multicolor, 70
  "personality" of, 74, 79
  radial print, 78
  selection of, 68-70, 108
  solid color, 70
  stripe print, 87, 146
  too short, 102
Fabric chart, 110, 113, 117, 121, 125
Fabri-Solvy, 86
Fan border, 66
Fans, 45–46, 59
Feathered spokes, 33, 141
Five-sided spiral templates, 152
Florida 2007, 23, 44, 52
Flow gradation, 77
Flow settings, 59–60
Flowers, 58, 133
  broderie perse, 56
  pansies, 35
  roses, 57, 108
Flying Tumbleweeds, 57
Foundation Stuff, 86
Foundations, 82-86
  leave-in, 106
  material for, 82-86, 148
  paper, 103
  removable, 103-104
  spiral, 84-85
  tear-away, 86,106
Fourth of July, 52
Free setting, 57–58
Fruit Salad Spinner, 143
Fun-dation non-woven
    foundation sheets, 86
Fussy-cut fabric, 87, 122, 132, 146

G

Gingkoesque, 52
*Goodness Gracious, Great Ball
    of Fire!*, 15, 138
Gradations, 70, 72, 75–77, 79
  changing, 50-51

Grandpa Shirts, 40

H
Hand-quilting, 104
Hanging sleeve, 127
Hearts Form From Pieces, 62
Holiday Whirl, 24, 52
Hot & Cold, 59

I
In Memory of Marja, 133
Increments, 11, 14, 22, 42-43
Infinite Rainbow, 128
Inks, testing, 83
Internet resources, 7, 145
Interrupted spokes, 32
Intersections, crossing, 94
Irregular shapes, 10, 35
Irregular spirals, 46
It's My Bag, 71

J
Jade Crystals, 37
Jinzenji, Yoshiko, 130
Joining, 45–51

K
Kaleidoscope Kreator, 53
Kaleidoscopic effects, 32, 53, 59
Kicker color, 68

L
Laser toner, 83
Leave-in foundations, 86
Lightweight Pellon, 86, 104
Lightweight muslin or organza, 86

M
Machine-quilting, 90, 104
Majestic Mandalai—A Personal Journey, 46, 140
Mandalas, 63
Markers, 82
Mesclun Mixed, 45
Midsummer, 36, 64
Midwinter, 65
Mistakes, fixing, 94, 101–102
Multiple interrupted spokes, 32

Multiple spirals, 59
Multiple-shape flow setting, 60, 64–65
Muslin, lightweight, 86
My Bloomin' Spiral, 56

N
Needles, for sewing machine, 90
Nesting spirals, 9, 12–15, 31, 108–111
    connecting, 48–49
    drawing, 12–15
    sewing, 94–95
    variations, 12
Next-Step trim, 93
Nine-patch blocks, 116-119
Non-spiral elements, 57
Northern Stars, 36, 50
Not My Dad's Bow Ties, 51, 61

O
Off-center spirals, 42–43
Organza, lightweight, 86
Oriental Fantasy, 66
Over the Rainbow, 40, 132–133
Overlap spirals, 58

P
Paper, 82, 86
Paper foundations, 82-86, 103-104
Partial spirals, 38–39
Partial-seam piecing, 22, 26, 98-99,114
Pattern
    in color and fabric, 68, 70, 79
    gradation of, 75
    size/scale, 74
Peeking Spirals, 8, 39
Pellon, 83–86, 104
Pencils, mechanical, 82
Pens, 82–83
Perspective, creating, 42–43, 75
Photo Op?!, 129
Photocopying templates, 84
Pictorial centers, 52
Pieced centers, 52
Piecing, thickness of, 104
Pineapple design, 35
Pinning fabric, 91, 103

Pinwheel spirals, 9, 20–23, 31, 34, 44, 53, 1386, 140
    connecting, 47
    drawing, 20–23
    sewing, 96–98
Plum Crazy, 53
Points, 45–46, 59, 92, 101
    bulky, 47
Point-to-Point spirals, 9, 31, 24–27, 112–114, 120–123
    connecting, 47
    drawing, 24–27
    sewing, 96–98
Prairie Breezes, 54
Pressing, 95, 104
Pringle, Lucy, 135
Printable foundation sheets, 83–86
Printers, inkjet or laser, 83-86
Problems and solutions, 101–102
Projects, 106-127
Proportions, of spirals, 10, 18
Purple Spiral #1 (Down the Drain), 20, 28, 54

Q
Quilters, online, 7
Quilting, 104

R
Rainbow, double, 128
Random increments, 43
Resources, 145
Rhinestone pin, as center, 58
Ribbons, 46, 59
Ribbons of Life, 62
Rings, 11, 22, 34–35
    coloring variations in, 36
    gradation through, 77
Rinse-away foundations, 83-86
Roses Are My Best Friends, 57
Rotary cutter, 88
Ruby beholder, 69
Ruler, 88
Rules, breaking, 38–39

S
Sails & Waves, 39, 50–51, 136
Sashing, 18, 49

Sawtooth edges, 22, 44, 99–100
Scale, in fabric, 70, 74
Scissors, 88
Seam rollers, 90
Seams
  allowances, 88, 103
  bulky, 103
  removing, 100
  trimming and pressing, 93
Secondary colors, 70, 72–73
Separation, of fabric and color, 68, 71, 73, 79
Settings, 56–61
Sewing techniques, 81, 91, 92–105
Sewing machine preparation, 90
Shapes, for spirals, 10, 59
Shards, 37
Simple Foundations Translucent Vellum Paper, 83-86
Single setting, 56
Single Spiral design, 30
Single-shape flow setting, 59–60
Six-sided spiral templates, 152–153
Smooth spokes, 30, 33
Snail's Trail block, 16
Snowflakes, 46, 144
Software, 53
Solid centers, 52
Spin, changing direction of, 40–41, 60
Spiral borders, 66–67
Spiral Comparison Chart, 31
Spiral of Life, 131
Spiral Pansies, 35
Spiraling Roses on My Table, 108–111
Spirals, 9–11. *See also* Baravelle spirals; Nesting spirals; Pinwheel spirals; Point-to-Point spirals
  centers of, 11, 50, 52–54
  connecting, 45–51, 103-104
  designing with, 29–79
  drawing, 9, 12–27
  enhancing, 78
  multiple, 59
  overlap, 58
  partial, 38–39
  sewing techniques for, 81, 91,

94–106
  shapes for, 10
  size of, 84
  templates for, 148-156
  within spirals, 64–65
Spiro Pony From Texas, 58
Spiromaniacs Blog, The, 7, 128
Splish Splash Spirals, 42–43, 52, 134
Split flow gradation, 77
Split points and fans, 45
Spokes, 11
  blending and separating, 72–73
  double, 32, 126
  feathered, 33, 143
  gradation in and across, 77
  interrupted, 32
  smooth, 30, 33
  variations, 32–33
Square spiral templates, 150–151
Squares and diamonds, 62
Starry Night, 46, 54, 69
Stitches, tension and length, 92
Stitching tips, 92
Straightedge/ruler, 82
Strip method of cutting, 89
Structure, of fabrics, 74
Style, of fabrics, 74
Sunbursts, 36
Surrounds, 55
Sustenance, 58
Symmetrical shapes, 10
Synergy, 46, 49, 124–127

T
Tannenbaum Twist, 115 Tape removal, 92
Tape, 82, 88, 90-91
Tear-Easy, 83-86
Template method of cutting, 88
Templates, 6, 84-85, 109, 143, 148–156
  time-savers, 87
Tension, of thread, 90
Texture, addition of, 70
Theme, and fabrics, 68, 74
Thread, for sewing machine, 90
Toner, testing, 83-86

Tools
  for cutting fabric, 88
  for foundation making, 82–83, 86
  for sewing, 90
  for trimming, 93
  sources for, 145
Tree Canopy, 38
Triangle spiral templates, 148-149
Triangles, 11, 101
Trimming seams, 93
Tropicale, 63
Trunks, 45, 51, 59
Twelve-sided spiral template, 156
Twisted Log Cabin block, 20
Twisting Ribbons border, 67

U
Untitled (Red, White & Black), 34, 58

V
Value, of colors, 68–69, 71, 73, 76
Value placement, 71
Variations, 12, 16, 20, 24, 31–33, 36, 42–44
Vellum sheets, 83–86
Vestments for St. Bart's, 46, 67
Vroom! Vroom!, 52, 55

W
Wandering lines, 38
We're Not In Kansas Anymore!, 79, 139
We've Got Sisters, 100
Websites, 7, 145
Whirlpool Galaxy, A Glorious Creation, 71
Whirlygig, 141
Winged Water, 33

Y
"Y" seams, 103
Yardage, calculating, 87, 146–147

Z
Zowie! Powie!, 120–123

Take Your Quilting Skills to New Heights

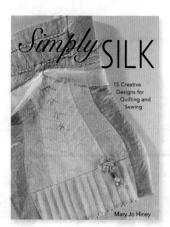

Simply Silk:
12 Creative Designs for Quilting and Sewing
by Mary Jo Hiney

*U*ncover the mystery and diminish the fear of working with silk, and learn to transform this delicate fabric into a top choice material for all kinds of projects and techniques.

Paperback; 128 pages
ISBN-13: 978-0-89689-548-5
ISBN-10: 0-89689-548-3
Item# Z0974

Spinning Pinwheel Quilts:
Curved Piecing Using the 3-6-9 Design System
by Sara Moe

*U*sing the fun, pinless and foolproof 3-6-9 Design System, you'll discover endless quilt design possibilities within your reach. Includes bonus CD featuring appliqué templates and embroidery designs.

paperback; 128 pages
ISBN-13:978-0-89689-559-1
ISBN-10: 0-89689-559-9
Item# Z0996

No-Stress Paper Piecing:
13 Projects Using Flannel or Cotton
by Carolyn Cullinan McCormick

*G*ain insider instruction for using easy-to-follow techniques and the essential Add-A-Quarter™ tools to incorporate flannel and cotton fabrics into your paper-piecing quilt projects. Contains a CD with 13 projects, including lap and baby quilts.

Paperback; 128 pages
ISBN-13: 978-0-89689-493-8
ISBN-10: 0-89689-493-2
Item# Z0764

Quilt as Desired:
Your Guide to Straight-Line and Free-Motion Quilting
by Charlene C. Frable

*T*ake your quilting skills to new heights with the six projects, using straight-line and free-motion techniques, featured in this revolutionary new guide. Discover what it means to truly quilt as desired.

Hardcover, 128 pages
ISBN-13: 978-0-89689-479-2
ISBN-10: 0-89689-479-7
Item# Z0743